DISCOVERING the QUALITY of SUCCESS

DISCOVERING the QUALITY of SUCCESS

**Success is not in never falling
but in rising every time you fall.**

Paul H. Dunn

compiled by
GARY GOUGH
and
JERIL WINGET

DESERET BOOK COMPANY
Salt Lake City, Utah
1977

Lithographed by

DESERET PRESS

in the United States of America

Foreword

It is difficult to write about success, for in doing so one implies that he is successful and that he has all the answers just waiting for someone to read them. No one has all the answers, but in this book, *Discovering the Quality of Success*, our father-in-law, Elder Paul H. Dunn, offers some of his own discoveries and formulas for success. We feel that he has much to say that is worthwhile and practical for today's youth.

Since Elder Dunn became a General Authority, his popularity among young people has been overwhelming. He has a spiritual insight and a zest for life that appeal to youth, and he is able to talk with them about their problems with great understanding and patience. Indeed, we feel that he has found the key to unlock any generation gap that may exist between youth and adults.

Youth today are concerned about the future and their success in that future. Many wonder what life has in store for them. Some see nothing but darkness and confusion. Yet Elder Dunn recognizes there is a bright light ahead, and it is this bright light of success through gospel living that forms the basis of the writings in this volume.

If there is one theme that characterizes the messages in this book, it is Elder Dunn's oft-quoted admonition, "Success is not in never falling, but in rising every time you fall."

It has been our pleasure to work with Elder Dunn in the compilation of *Discovering the Quality of Success*. We feel that the chapters represent him at his best, and we commend them to you. We feel his skillful use of stories enhances the gospel messages contained herein.

We are confident that this book is one that you will want to read again and again, for its message is both stimulating and enjoyable.

May we add our witness that the wisdom and counsel within these pages can truly make anyone aspire to discover the quality of success and to achieve life's ultimate goal—that of successful living.

Gary R. Gough
Jeril D. Winget

I gratefully acknowledge the encouragement and assistance of my two sons-in-law, Gary Gough and Jeril Winget, in the preparation of this book.

They are both examples of discovering success.

CONTENTS

CHAPTER 1

Three Ingredients for Success

Some time ago I was delighted to listen to an educator who listed three basic ingredients for ultimate success in life. They would certainly apply to total living. They are not new. There is no new revelation that I am going to bring to your attention. But these are ingredients that work!

Development of Native Capacities

The first basic ingredient this educator related was the need for ultimate *development of our native capacities*— the endowment that we have received from on high as it relates to our talents and abilities. We teach the world that all mankind is literally the offspring of an eternal Heavenly Father. We are brothers and sisters in an eternal family. And in our understanding of gospel principles, we can fully appreciate that in coming to mortality as we have, we bring with us that innate ability to reach the top in whatever we desire to do.

I think we can appreciate too, in order not to over-simplify the gospel program, that there are many differing abilities and capacities. We are not alike. I think this is obvious in many scriptures. But I would hasten to add that each of us has within himself the power and the capacity to become like our Heavenly Father and Mother, which suggests to me that whatever our interests and abilities might be, when they are properly developed and we are properly motivated, we can in reality be perfect. That suggests to me that in an educational environment there is no such thing as a failing student. I appreciate that, where there are many differences, each must find himself. That is one of the reasons we have the programs aligned in our great educational institutions—to assist one another in tapping the abilities that we have.

I do not believe for a moment that we are all destined to be great brain surgeons or lawyers or artists, but we have within us the ability to succeed in life—to accomplish whatever we wish in whatever our field of pursuit might be.

I notice as I travel throughout the Church, and particularly as the student element seeks counsel, that discouragement and concern in the field of educational pursuits often lead the list of problems. Sometimes this area of discouragement almost invalidates the inner capacity that we have.

Someone has said that success consists not in never falling, but in rising every time you fall. There will always be many discouraging factors that enter the productive periods of our lives as we seek for ultimate perfection, but if we can get up one time more than we go down, we will always win. Life is problem solving, and in solving our problems we grow and mature and develop. We are here to experience.

Another has said that there are dozens of rules for success, but none of them work unless we do. There is a lot in that, because frequently we become our own greatest barriers. The capacity, in other words, is within us, but what we do with it depends on each individual. This principle, of course, is one of the greatest in the gospel, and keeping it foremost in our minds helps to lead us in the right direction.

Sometimes in the educational environment, because we are not perfect in our total understanding of people, we tend to measure each other in very inaccurate terms. This comes into focus with the various testing programs that are available to all of us in any institution of higher learning. At best, these programs are only barometers of our interests and abilities.

May I be so bold as to suggest that in any teaching situation I have found that if I can develop enough basic interest and motivation in a student, then that student can achieve in any field that he or she so desires. So I think the key is in our interest and motivating factors—not so much in the basic intelligence that might be expressed in a rather inaccurate test. In other words, you already have all the potential that you need. The question is, "Will you keep the interest and the motivation secure enough to ultimately develop that which is yours?"

This becomes one of the challenges of our teaching profession, of our administrations—to create in each student an ultimate desire to set high attainable goals.

I am interested in this statement:

> *People don't fail due to lack of knowledge, but rather because they fail to use the knowledge that they have. Applied knowledge is the knowedge that pays off. Application is the key. We are dealing with mortals—people who are personalities. It is important that we adapt our special knowledge and become aware of what is successful in our own experiences. There is no one best way for all men. There may be, however, a highly successful method for you. Add your individual touch. Create your own image.*

Be yourself as you discover this image in this marvelous environment. I think there is a great deal of truth in that.

Opportunity

The second basic ingredient of success is *opportunity*. Assuming that we are properly motivated in the first area, the second almost naturally unfolds. Someone has said:

> *Two men look out*
> *Through the self-same bars.*
> *One sees the mud,*
> *The other the stars.*

It is a matter of point of view.

Opportunity is all about us. One of the processes that you are experiencing in life is creating your own opportunities. Much could be said here. I think that unfortunately many Latter-day Saints tend to fall prey to the mediocre life—they have created little or no opportunity because they haven't fully capitalized on the talents and abilities they possess.

As an institute coordinator in southern California I was privileged to be on some seventy different college campuses from time to time. It became quite well known that I was working with the college element. Thus, when both Latter-day Saint and nonmember business and industry leaders were looking for capable, dedicated people to hire, it was natural for them to call one who had daily contact with this trained element. No less than five or ten times a week I would receive telephone calls from some of the finest men in southern California wanting to know about college students.

I had in my desk almost continually job opportunities in more than fifty different categories. Do you know what my greatest problem was? I couldn't find enough young men qualified to fill them. Here is the paradox in our modern society—in any given week I would have five to ten college-age people walk into my office and say, in essence, "Brother Dunn, do you know where I can get a good job—a high-paying job?"

I would open up the drawer and bring out my list and say, "Yes. Can you qualify?" There often followed this answer, "No." Here were young men with all the capacities and abilities in the world, but they hadn't taken the opportunity to develop them to their fullest. I suppose if anything pained my heart, it was to see young men and young women terminate their education too soon because they lacked the vision to see what was ahead in the immediate future.

The vice-president of a great corporation in the southern California region called me. As he identified himself, he said, "We have never met, Mr. Dunn, but I know a great deal about your program and your people, and I am so impressed with the philosophy and the point of view that your group represents that I would like to fill six junior executive positions with your people. I will take any six that you send over to me, sight unseen, providing, number one, they have a bachelor's degree or its equivalent." We spelled out what he meant by *equivalent* in terms of other experiences and exposure to educational programs.

Then I paused to ask him, "Do you want some specific area of concentration—liberal arts, engineering, mathematics orientation? What do you need?"

He said, "It doesn't matter. Industry today will specifically train the individual in these areas of detail. What we want is a person with a broad point of view who has been exposed to the educational processes—one who can solve problems without asking for advice every few minutes." Securing an education teaches us how to think and to rationalize and to apply principles, and this is the same procedure used in business.

I said, "Fine. Thank you. What's the second point?"

He said, "That you recommend without reservation the moral character of the individual whom you send. Is he honest, true, and moral? If he can pass those two tests, Mr. Dunn, he has the job."

Then he spelled out the job detail. The minimum position started at $6,500 a year (then a good starting salary). It carried with it a brand new car and $30 a month lunch money. The higher the man's educational attainment, the higher the beginning salary was. My own appetite was whetted!

The sad part of this story is that from seventy college campuses, I could get only two of the positions filled. Within two to three weeks of this experience, however, I had in my office no less than twenty-five returned missionaries who had left school seeking the opportunity of a lifetime. They were somewhat concerned as to why people would not take them on and give them all of the rewards of life. Isn't it interesting?

Industry indicates to all of us that at the top in any field of endeavor the vacancy sign is always posted. In the middle ranks and at the lower end, the semiskilled or the nonskilled positions, we have no opening because too many have already qualified. At the top in your field are opportunities galore, and the door is wide open. You have it in you—you have the ability, and the opportunity is waiting.

The Will to Serve

Now, third, the *will to serve.* I suppose that of all of these this point becomes the most vital and important, and yet it cannot be looked at apart from the other two.

The attitude that the Lord has revealed to all of us in the restored gospel of Jesus Christ is the forgetting of self —willingly giving of that which we have to others. That is easy to say, but it is a very difficult thing to practice. It is easy to talk about but another thing to do.

Between my baseball and army careers and affiliation in Church education, I spent ten years in my father's grocery business, eventually becoming the manager of one of the new supermarkets we opened in southern California. It was the typical supermarket that you are familiar with. I had 35 employees in this store, and I had an opportunity over a number of years to visit with many others who sought employment in this particular industry— to say nothing, of course, of the young teenagers who wanted part-time or summer jobs.

I wish there were a practical way that in our educational institutions we could have every student sit in the position of the employer, to see themselves as they really are. I think you are aware of those things that you normally would want to know as you seek a job. How much does it pay? (That will be asked within the first two minutes, if not sooner.) What are the fringe benefits? How many breaks during the day? When do I come? And how soon do I get out of here? (That's the best way I know to have your application go to the bottom of the pile. And yet young people frequently use this approach.)

About three or four weeks after we had our grand opening at the market I managed, I was plagued with applications for employment. It was a hard time in the late 1940s, and it was obvious that there were fewer jobs than the number of people seeking them.

I got a telephone call one afternoon from a sixteen-year-old high school boy. He was very much to the point —very polite—and radiated just enough self-confidence that I wanted to listen for a moment. He used the right terminology—he always said "yes, sir" and let me take the lead.

The young man said, "Mr. Dunn, you don't know me, but I have watched with great interest the opening of your fine market in our community. My mother has been a constant shopper there ever since and she is delighted!"

I don't know how delighted she really was, but I was ready to hear more.

He said, "I realize that you probably have all of your positions filled, but I believe I have something that will help your business. At a time that is convenient to you, sir, I would like to present my credentials. May I?" A sixteen-year-old boy!

I wanted to hear more about him. I said, "How about Wednesday afternoon after school?"

"Yes, sir, I'll be there." So we set an appointment for four o'clock.

At one minute to four, here came this young man, properly dressed and with a certain amount of confidence in his walk. I am sure he was scared to death. He probably had more butterflies than most of us have as he approached this interview. Then, as I watched this little episode unfold, I thought, "Wouldn't it be marvelous if our deacons and teachers and priests could dress like this on Sunday and walk with equal competence and confidence?"

As we walked into the office, I had him take a seat. I pulled up a chair beside him and said, "Tell me just a little bit about yourself."

He said, "I have had experience as a box boy on Saturdays. I believe I know enough of the business to be an asset to your organization. In fact, I have something that you need!"

I said, "Oh? What's that?"

He answered, "Service. Mr. Dunn, I don't expect you

to believe that but, because I do have some ability, I'd like to prove it to you. May we step out into the store for just a moment?"

I said, "Why, certainly."

So we did and he took me over to the wall where all the canned goods were lined up. In opening the store we were having a difficult time keeping the shelves properly stocked.

He said, "Now, Mr. Dunn, I think you know enough about sales appeal and the intuition of women as they shop around in a store to realize that if that shelf could always look full and properly aligned, you could probably increase your sales. I'm the greatest boy in the world in terms of keeping shelves stocked. I don't expect you to believe that either. You even look a little doubtful, but would you be willing to let me invest one week of my time every afternoon after school and all day Saturday to show you what I can do? And you have no obligation, sir."

What do you imagine I was thinking? At that time I had five part-time box boys, and they were all the "let's-see-what-time-we-can-get-out-of-here" boys. These kids would always gather at the counter with their friends. They were more concerned about acceptance with their peer group than they were about what they could give to a business. They had the capacity, but they lacked the will to serve and to give of themselves.

Now if you were managing a store, which element would you want? Do I have to tell you what I did? I had him take his coat off and show me. He worked that one afternoon, and I didn't need to watch him very long. I let three boys go the next Saturday, because this young man could fill all three positions.

Was the opportunity there? Maybe it wasn't obvious, but he created one. He had the ability, but more important he had the will to give and to serve and to show to the world in an unselfish way what he could do.

Who do you think got the consistent raises? Whom do you think I made openings for in the future as the store volume dropped and settled to normal? Who do you think was going to succeed in college? Who do you think was going to the top in business with an attitude like this? There is no question!

You have the ability and you have the opportunity in the world awaiting. If you can couple those two with a willing desire to serve and give of yourself in an unselfish manner, there is no question in my mind where you will be five, ten, or fifteen years from now. You will be literally a leader of business and of industry and of the Church and of the community. This philosophy is the thing that I think the Lord is trying to get us to see in His program—the practical way to build happy and secure lives here, now, and forever.

Someone has said, "I know of no great man except those who have rendered great service to the human race." And service can be involved in all capacities of dealing with people in and out of the Church.

May the Lord help you not only to tap to the fullest extent the capacities that you have, but to give willingly in the spirit of the gospel.

CHAPTER 2

Plan to Be Great

A used-car salesman wanted to buy a cow because his family had increased in sufficient numbers to warrant it. So he went to a farmer who had an extra cow and who had bought a car from him six months previously. The farmer listed the purchase sale of his wonderful animal, and the invoice read: "Basic cow, $200. Two-tone exterior, $45. Extra stomach, $75. Product storage compartment, $60. Four dispensing devices, $10 each. Genuine cowhide upholstery, $125. Dual horns, $15. Automatic flyswatter, $35. Total price of cow, $595." I think that shows creativity and originality. Originality is basic to success.

Meetings and Involvement

My ears are always open when I travel from place to place, because sometimes great sermons are created from observations and conversations we make with one another. Coming into the chapel one weekday evening, I overheard someone say, "Here we go to another meeting." We are a meeting people and for a good reason. I suppose one might sometimes question the wisdom of keeping us so involved, but there is wisdom in it.

I mentioned a little verse once that goes like this:

> *One day for church, six days for fun—*
> *Odds on going to heaven, six to one.*

We can reduce those odds by being in church. My dad penned a little verse that was similar. He said:

> *Whenever I pass our little ward,*
> *I linger for a visit.*
> *So when I'm carried in,*
> *The Lord won't say, "Who is it?"*

It is nice to get acquainted with the Lord and his program.

That reminds me of still another experience that I had in company with President Hugh B. Brown. We were flying together to Los Angeles to hold a special meeting with some returned missionaries. We had no sooner become airborne when he leaned over to me and said, "Paul, do you realize that we're so involved in Church work that we really can't take credit for any of the good that we're doing?"

I guess a little concern showed on my face, for he said, "Do you realize it is almost impossible for you and me to sin? So we can't really take the credit. Almost everybody knows us, and therefore we wouldn't dare sin even if we thought about it."

I guess I still looked puzzled. About that time a stewardess walked by, and President Brown said, "Young lady, would you bring this young man and me a cup of coffee?"

I thought, "Good heavens, what now!"

She put her hands on her hips and said, "I will not. I know who you are and you can't have it."

He asked, "Who am I?"

She replied, "You're President Brown of the Mormon Church. I'll get you some Seven-up."

He asked, "Are you a member of our faith?"

She replied, "No, but I know who you are, and you still can't have it."

As she went to prepare the Seven-ups, President Brown nudged me and with a smile said, "You see what I mean. We can't even commit a sin." That's what good example does. Attendance at Church meetings can assist us in learning "how to act." The purpose of meetings and involvement, then, is to help people.

Here is what the Lord told the Prophet Joseph Smith about meetings:

> And now, behold, I give unto you a commandment, that when ye are assembled together ye shall instruct and edify each other, that ye may know how to act and direct my church, how to act upon points of my law and commandments, which I have given.
>
> And thus ye shall become instructed in the law of my church, and be sanctified by that which ye have received, and ye shall bind yourselves to act in all holiness before me—
>
> That inasmuch as ye do this, glory shall be added to the kingdom which you have received. Inasmuch as ye do it not, it shall be taken, even that which ye have received. (D&C 43:8-11.)

What Makes People Great?

Basically, I am a very lazy fellow and will just glide if given half an opportunity. (I notice that I have lots of company in the world!) I find that I have to set goals in order to keep my mind fresh and my life progressing. Writing books helps me research and learn. One of the things I am trying to do in my research is find out what makes people great. What are the basic ingredients that cause a Colonel

Irwin to be an astronaut who succeeds in life? Did you notice the failures that he encountered in his life as he made his upward climb? Every life has its setbacks. Falling down is no disgrace; it is the getting up that makes the champion. Get up one time more than you fall, and you will always succeed.

When I wanted to be a ball player some years ago, a great high school coach taught me a principle. When I went in to sign up as a freshman, he asked, "Do you want to be a ball player or a champion?"

I replied, "I want to play ball."

He said, "If you just want to play ball, then you won't play here. But if you want to be a champion, you came to the right fellow—because I make champions, and a champion you will be." Isn't that a great thought!

Spiritually as well as academically I see thousands of great champions. Some are from the athletic world, some from the academic world, and some from the business world, the medical field, the science world, and all show that there are common denominators in building a successful life. Whether you are talking about Dr. Homer Warner, a great heart specialist; Robert Peterson of the Metropolitan Opera; or Harmon Killebrew or Vernon Law on the ball field, there are common denominators that create greatness. Let me give you three basic principles, ingredients if you please, that when applied and fully understood build greatness.

If I have one concern as I travel throughout the Church, it is for people who get discouraged and let discouragement prevent them from becoming great. There is no such word in the Mormon vocabulary as *can't*. There might be in your vocabulary *I won't* or *I'm not motivated* or *I don't care*, but there is no such word as *can't*, because you and I were born to succeed, and succeed we will.

When Coach Rupp, a great basketball coach, visited

Brigham Young University a few years ago, he declared, "Just remember that when you see a man on top of a mountain he didn't fall there." Success and greatness are processes of climbing, and climb you must. Would you just record these three ingredients:

Vision

First, champions have vision; they are visionary men. I do not mean that they see visions in the traditional theological sense, but they think big. They daydream like we daydream and plan. They have goals and great aspirations. If we could have a few hours with the astronaut, Colonel Irwin, he would tell us that as a little boy he was thinking about the future and that in his upward climb he, in a very delicate and consistent way, followed his plan, which one day brought him to that glorious moment on the moon. It did not just happen; he planned for it.

I notice that many times young people hope that success will occur in their lives. Whether you are thinking about professions, marriage, education, or military—whatever your concern at the moment—catch the whole vision. Plan for it. Orient your life accordingly. Get involved with people who can make that vision come true. If I were going to be a ball player again, I would go where ball players are. I would find out what ball players do and how they do it. I would learn every detail in and out until I became a ball player, and I would keep that vision before me.

Sometimes there are people who come into your life who mean to do right but use the wrong method. They become stumbling blocks. In general conference I once related that there were only five people in my life who really changed me, who took me from one plateau to a higher plateau. Thank God for those five! I have often wondered what would have happened to me if they had not been there. But I also met a few who did not inspire me. Sometimes those who do not inspire direct us in the wrong ways. These are the kinds of people who develop in us such things as *I can't* or *I won't.*

When I was in the fifth grade in Arkansas, for example, I used to daydream a lot. (I did in all the grades, but this one in particular!) One day right after lunch I was thinking big during an English class. Have you ever had (pardon me, English teachers) English right after lunch? English was not particularly exciting to me, so I was daydreaming. I was looking out the window and thinking big. I actually was planning the ceremony to induct me into the Hall of Fame. You should have been there. It was one of the greatest ceremonies the world has ever witnessed.

The teacher, seeing a wayward boy in her charge, did what she thought was best and, in order to bring me back to reality, called on me. (I question that method of bringing a person back to reality, but she preferred to use it!) She said, *"Paul Dunn, come up here!"*

I walked to the front of the room. The teacher handed me a piece of chalk and said, "Diagram this sentence on the board!"

I looked at the chalk; I looked at the board; I looked at the sentence; and then I walked over and drew a square around the sentence.

She said, "I thought so. Come here!"

I walked over, and she turned me around and had me face the class. Putting those eaglelike claws on my shoulders, she said, "Class, I have been teaching English in this school for over thirty years. (I think that was part of her problem!) Without a doubt, this is the dumbest boy I have ever had!"

Now that does not build confidence. It was a barrier! I took a silent oath and covenant that I would never take another book home—and I didn't. Who paid the price? I did, not the school district, although in a sense the community suffered too because a little boy was discouraged.

We must contend with people like that in our lives. But we must keep thinking big and know by right of our theology that we are born to succeed in this life. We must also think big as far as the Church is concerned.

Sometimes you are put on the spot just because of who you are. You find lots of critics in the world, and as you share your Latter-day Saint identification with others, it becomes a challenge. In a sense I am grateful for this, because you will show your true colors—whether or not you can stand up and be counted.

I have always appreciated being put on the spot, because it makes me remember who I am and certain covenants that I have made. Do you know what this Church really is? It is the most glorious organization the world has ever known, and, of course, it is the kingdom of God restored to earth. Sometimes, when you get into academic environments, people tend to criticize the Church and its programs. If you are not careful and if you do not have the vision, it is easy to become critical yourself.

Let me share an experience that happened while I was presiding over the New England Mission some years ago. My mission office was located two blocks from Harvard campus, one block from Radcliffe, two and a half miles from MIT, three miles from Boston College, and four miles from Boston University. Wellesley College was not far away, and many other schools of equal competence were nearby in this Boston environment. Looking outside my office window, I could see the Henry W. Longfellow home and estate. I used to sit at my desk occasionally and look out the window and just meditate.

On one occasion as I was doing a little thinking and daydreaming when about twenty-five Harvard-Radcliffe students rounded the corner of Longfellow Park and headed toward the mission office. The group was barefoot and, for the most part, dressed in clothes that looked as if they were out trick or treating. The were carrying placards that read, "Feed the starving children of Biafra."

I was surprised when they entered the mission office. I could hear my secretary having a little challenge, and then the intercom rang and he said," "President, I've got some college students here who say they will not go until you see them."

I said, "Bring them in."

As I opened the door, in came twenty-five of the most interesting-looking college students I had seen in a long time. I offered them each a chair, but they thought that was too much like the Establishment. They preferred to sit on the floor.

A big burly fellow with a large bushy beard and hair to match was their spokesman. He said, "Dr. Dunn, we have done a little research on you and your church, and we don't think you represent true Christianity. You and your church are racists! We're here to correct it. We will not leave your office, sir, until you personally donate $500 to the children of Biafra."

What would you have done? I thought I could pick up the phone and call the law enforcement agencies. But what would the Savior have done? He would probably teach them, would He not? He would educate. So I declared, "That's fascinating. I'm delighted to see that I'm going to be so generous. Before I donate my $500, would you be willing to answer a few questions?"

"Certainly," was the reply.

"You all look intelligent," I said, "and you're out for a worthy cause. Let me ask you a few questions." I looked at the big burly fellow on the floor and said, "May I ask any one of you since you're all here in a common cause?"

He replied, "Certainly."

I moved third row over to the corner where there was a skinny girl who did not have much on. I said, "Young lady, would you stand up, please? Yes, you. Stand, please."

She stood up, and I said, "I happen to know a little about administrative affairs. I know that when people donate money, there sometimes is a creaming off. I'm interested in knowing into whose hands my check goes and how many of my dollars actually go to Biafra. Would you walk me through the administrative distribution of my check please?"

She answered, "I don't even know who we're going to turn it over to."

I didn't think she did, and so I said, "Thank you. Would you be seated?"

Then I picked out a little fellow and said, "Would you stand, sir?"

He stood up, and I asked, "Where are you in school?"

He replied, "I'm a Harvard sophomore."

"What's your major?"

"Economics." (He looked as if he needed it!)

I said, "I understand that you're here on a Harvard scholarship (this had come out in our discussion). Would you mind telling me what Harvard, with its massive endowment, and you personally are doing for the Maori people?"

He replied, "Who are the Maoris?"

Then I told him who the Maoris were and gave him a little Church history. (Do you know who the Maoris are and what our Church has done for these great people in New Zealand over the last hundred-plus years? Do you have the whole vision, or are you caught in a little academic corner somewhere, saying, "Yeah, we are kind of an odd group.")

I called on another fellow and said, "Would you stand, please?"

As he stood I inquired, "Would you tell me what your university and you personally are doing for the children of Samoa?"

He did not know and replied, "I'm not doing anything personally."

I asked, "Would you like to know what the Mormon Church is doing in Samoa?"

"Yes, sir," was the reply.

So I taught him.

Then I asked him, "Where were you in 1967 when the hurricane hit?"

"I was in high school," he replied.

I said, "Do you want to know where the Mormon Church was? I was coordinating that part of the world when word came to me from a great mission president that food, medicine, water, and supplies were needed. Within twenty-four hours crucial supplies were bought by the tithing and fast offerings of our people to save not just the Mormons, but thousands of natives who were homeless. I noticed that Harvard University and even a Red Cross unit were not there."

Calling on another student, I said, "What are you doing with your personal funds for the people of Tonga?"

He did not know, and so I taught a similar story. I asked him about the Tahitian children, and then told the group about the elementary school system that members of our Church support with their tithing.

I walked him through the great Lamanite program. "What are Harvard and Radcliffe and MIT doing to help the Lamanites, the starving American Indians?" And as I inquired, they did not know. So once more I taught them one of the great programs of the Church—to say nothing of welfare and other social agencies at work. They were becoming more humble with each experience.

Finally, I said, "I'll tell you what I'll do. I have my checkbook here. I will sign a personal check for $500 for the children of Biafra if collectively you will all donate $500 to the Mormon Church to help the needy kids of the Pacific." I have never seen twenty-five students exit an office so fast in my life.

What did I learn on this occasion and many occasions like it? These students were not out for a cause— they were caught up, for the most part, in a rebellious movement. Ninety-five percent of those young people did not even know what they were rebelling for. Of course, there are some great causes, but are you aware of what your Church is doing throughout the world? Can you stand up and be counted? Can you teach the rest of the world? You do not have to take a backseat to anybody.

I notice when all these great deeds are being performed, the news media throughout the world are not telling the world how the Church helps and educates people. But the minute there is a little activity that is not understood, we get publicity galore. Keep the vision of who you are and what this great Church is really accomplishing.

Preparation

Secondly, I notice that great people, regardless of their fields of endeavor, are prepared. We too must be prepared—that is why we become educated. I don't mean only preparation in the skills of your trade, but also spiritual preparation. This is what formal education is all about, what Church meetings are all about. We are not just meeting in Church to have another meeting. We are meeting to learn how to live and how to give of ourselves as we go forth to make great decisions.

There are wonderful assignments waiting for you in the world. The world is looking to you for spiritual as well as academic direction. If we have a problem, it is simply that we cannot be trained fast enough, diligently enough, and thoroughly enough. Do you want to sit in the highest seat of your profession? It is open, if you are qualified. But this takes preparation, and this Church is synonymous with being prepared.

Enthusiasm

Thirdly, enthusiasm is paramount in the lives of the most successful people with whom I have been acquainted.

The one thing that kills interest is lack of enthusiasm. You can do anything you want if you are enthusiastic about it. Someone has said that if you will look enthusiastic and act enthusiastic, you will be enthusiastic.

I am in the process of learning a verse that reads:

> It's only the view from where you sit
> That makes you feel defeat.
> Life is full of many aisles,
> So why don't you change your seat?

Get that vision! Move over and see life from a different perspective!

As I visited with Harmon Killebrew one time, I asked him, "What makes for greatness?"

He talked about this preparation and enthusiasm almost in the same voice.

I said, "Look, Harm, I think the world knows that you had never seen a major league ball game, let alone played in one, until you signed a major league contract. How did you do it?"

He replied, "You have to make your own opportunity. After school and work, I would go practice, practice, practice. That makes for good preparation."

One day it came to the attention of Herman Welker, the senator from Idaho, that there was a kid in the sandlots of Payette, Idaho, who was hitting potatoes farther than professional baseball players were hitting balls. He brought this to the attention of Clark Griffith, owner of the Washington Senators. Ozzie Bluege, the great baseball scout, was sent to look into the matter.

Unknown to Harm, the community arranged a local ball game, and Harmon Killebrew, a seventeen-year-old kid from a farm, hit a nine-inch, five-and-one-half-ounce baseball 435 feet (it rolled farther). The Senators signed him on that alone.

It took about four or five years' preparation with potatoes and old taped balls to get to the top. So when you see Killebrew hit a home run at an all-star game or in a World Series, remember what it took to make him ready. In addition to being prepared, he needed real enthusiasm.

I once had Harmon talk to my missionaries at a zone conference. After the conference we had a question-and-answer period. One fellow raised his hand and said, "Mr. Killebrew, I don't mean this to embarrass you, sir, but as a superstar, earning as much money as you do, what is the largest fine you have ever paid?"

I listened very carefully while this magnificent athlete leaned over, looked at the young men, and said, "I don't know. I haven't paid it yet."

Then I jumped up very quickly, put my arm around Harm, and said, "Harm, I've played a little ball myself. Would you mind telling this group what time a major league ball player is to report to the park for a night game?"

He replied, "Six o'clock."

I asked, "What time does Harmon Killebrew report?"

"Four," was his answer.

Do you want to know how to be a superstar? You prepare with enthusiasm. You start early and stay late!

I walked into the Portland, Oregon, airport one time to get something to eat. I opened a menu, and right across the top of the page in bold print was this statement: *HAVE YOU TRIED OUR ENTHUSIASTIC STEW?*

I hadn't, and so I called the waitress over and said, "What in the world is this?"

As she clenched her fists together, she said, "Oh, sir, order it!"

I asked, "But what in the world is it?"

She replied, "Sir, that's a stew we put everything we've got into!"

I ordered it, and she was right.

That is what the gospel is all about—you put everything you have into it. Everything! You do not hold anything back. Are you enthused about the Church? Are you enthused about life? Are you enthused about the gospel? We ought to be the happiest people in the world. We have a message for eternity. You and I ought to bounce through life!

Be like my daughter Marsha was a few years ago when we moved from Hollywood to Downey, California. As we were unpacking, I did not notice Marsha crawl up on a half-made fence in the backyard. She saw several families four or five houses down, and she started to scream at them, "Hey, you people down there! Hey, all of you people down there!"

When I heard her, I ran into the yard to retrieve her. But before I could get there, she hollered, "Hey, you people! We're Mormons!" Are you as glad to be a Mormon?

Teach Your Neighbor

In our final days in Boston as our mission was drawing to a close, we were having an open house, and Billy Casper was kind enough to be our visitor to teach nonmembers.

One day before the meeting I was standing in a line at the Harvard Trust Company to close out our account. As I stood in line, I thought, "Whew! Ten minutes to relax."

Then the Spirit prompted me, "Paul, warn your neighbor."

I thought, "Oh, I am so tired!"

But the Spirit reminded me that I had been sent out for 1,095 days to warn thirteen million people.

Then I asked, "Who is my neighbor?"

The Spirit replied, "The guy in front of you." (Too often we warn our neighbor next door to death, but our neighbor is also the fellow whom we do not know.)

So I tapped this man on the shoulder. He turned around and said, "Yes?"

I asked, "Pardon me, sir, do you happen to be a Mormon bishop?" (Since he had a thin cigar in his hand, I didn't think he was.)

He said, "No, I'm not a Mormon bishop. Why do you ask?"

I replied, "I hope this isn't offensive to you, but you look like one."

He asked, "What does one look like?"

So I described a Mormon bishop.

This man was a sharp-looking young executive, thirty-five and well-dressed, and he seemed to know what he was doing and how to do it. When I finished describing a typical Mormon bishop, he said, "Well, thank you. I didn't know I projected that well."

I replied, "You really do."

We moved up a couple of spaces, and then I asked, "You play golf?"

He replied, "I'm a Sunday hacker."

"What's your handicap?"

"Thirteen"

I asked, "How would you like to reduce it?"

"Well," he replied, "who wouldn't?"

I said, "Do you know Bill Casper?"

"The golfer? Yes, I've heard of him," was the reply.

I said, "I've got him coming to a meeting tonight. Would you like to meet him?"

He said, "Believe I would."

So I took a card out of my pocket and wrote the mission address on it. Then I said, "You're my guest tonight. Seven o'clock."

That night when he arrived at the mission home, I introduced him to Billy Casper, and he thought that was great.

We had a tremendous meeting that evening, and before he left, I said, "You would not be offended if I had two young men call on you to teach you more, would you?"

He replied, "I'd be honored." He was baptized ninety days later—without the cigar. And he is going to be a great leader one day.

Gain a Testimony

There are some in our Church who still struggle—some who do not yet really know of the truth of the fullness of the gospel. Don't be embarrassed to say that you don't know.

Some have not been touched by the Spirit. Some have not really communicated with God. But you must be careful not to assign a limitation to God if you have not. Do not deprive some of us who have had a spiritual experience with the Lord from saying that He does live, because I testify that He does. The finite mind of man tends to assign a limitation to the infinite. There is danger in that, so be careful.

Try this little experiment. Put all the books you are now reading on educational and scientific subjects on one shelf, and then wait ten years and see how much truth is in them. (I would be embarrassed to take the textbook I used in the university and teach you with it now, because so much has changed.)

Then take the standard works of the Church and put them on another shelf. Do not wait ten years, but read them in the meantime. After ten years see how much they have not changed, and then ask yourself intellectually, "Where is truth?"

One Sunday morning when my Dad was twelve years old, he came home from priesthood meeting, walked into the kitchen, put his hands on his hips, and said, "Mom, guess what? I lost my testimony at priesthood this morning."

She said, "You what?"

He replied, "I lost my testimony in priesthood this morning."

She asked, "How did you do that?"

Then that young boy replied, "Our teacher said that all the spirits, every one of us, sat in the presence of God in a great council in heaven and voted on some things, part of which was the plan of salvation. I knew the Church wasn't true then, because I have sat in the Provo Tabernacle when I couldn't hear a speaker past the fourth row. So I knew God didn't really exist, because how can one person talk to an audience of billions?" (This was before the invention of the microphone!)

Do you see how a finite mind can assign a limitation to the infinite? What do you suppose Harold Dunn would have said if the priesthood leader had stated, "Come here, Harold I'm going to tell you a little story. In just a few short years you're going to have three sons and you'll name the middle one Paul. Paul is going to stand in the Tabernacle in Salt Lake City and give a talk that millions of people can hear." My father probably would have joined another church!

Do not get caught up in the thing you cannot always explain. This I can explain: God lives; Jesus is the Christ; this is His Church that has been restored. Some of us have been given a special witness. So while you struggle and fight and even occasionally get discouraged, have faith in those who know. Having trust and faith is one of the most important ingredients of success.

CHAPTER 3

The Quality of Learning

I have always been deeply impressed with an observation made by Plato. He said, "If a man's education is inadequate or bad, he becomes the most savage of all the products of earth." He points out the danger of finalizing one's education.

Bruce Barton said, "When we are through changing —we are through." Learning is an on-going process, and, as I see it, there is great danger of getting into the rut of closed minds at about age thirty. With all due respect to those who have passed that "magic mark," I say the *tendency* is for one to become secure and smug in that which he knows or has learned by that age, and it is most difficult to get a person to change his mind or point of view thereafter. As one clever wit said, "Some people are buried at seventy-five who were dead at thirty."

Teachers, lawyers, doctors, musicians, businessmen —those who have the natural ability to achieve great heights in their vocational work—often drift gradually into the background for the simple reason that they cannot see the need for constant growth. They think they have a corner on truth. They have broken the law of humility, and the law of humility is slowly but relentlessly breaking them. The only reason that God does not always help us to become more likable personalities, more beautiful characters, and more successful people is that we do not always ask with open minds and willing hearts for the necessary changes to be made.

St. Augustine was once asked what he considered to be the first word in the Christian philosophy of life. He replied, "Humility." And the second? "Humility." And the third? "Humility."

Jesus said, "Except ye be converted, and become as little children, ye shall not enter into the kingdom of heaven." (Matthew 18:3.) And the same may be said about the kingdom of science or music or law or business or any other field of physical activity. "Except ye become as little children—except you realize your own weakness and, with an open, teachable mind, go in search of new facts and added truths—ye shall not enter into the kingdom."

The Secret of Genius

There is a tendency for many of us to narrow our vision of the horizons and, in so doing, become restricted in educational exposure and experience. I was interested in reading a statement from Carlyle that I think is significant in this setting: "The secret of genius," he said, "is to carry the spirit of childhood into old age, with boundless curiosity about the future, flexibility, growing, hoping, trying, and ready at all times for any worthwhile change."

How Do You Do It?

I suppose the meaningful question is, "How do you progress?" This is the concern that I have, and in my own way I have found three things to be very helpful. They are not magic, but let me share them with you.

For many years I really struggled in trying to learn. Things do not come easy for me, and I find even to this time that I have to discipline myself in ways that might seem very peculiar to others in order to keep myself moving in the direction that I know I ought to go. Following are three steps to finding that learning can be delightful.

Be Consistent

First, read and learn something new every day! Don't let learning end with the end of a semester or next year's degree.

President McKay and Books

Several years ago the University of Utah put on a program to pay tribute to President McKay. I was given the assignment by the student committee to make the arrangements with President McKay.

On one occasion I was sitting with him talking about the program and noticed several new books on his desk. As I visited with him, I learned that he read through two or three books each day.

He said, as he glanced at one of the volumes, "I can hardly wait to get into this one."

He didn't read every word, but he had developed a system and a plan for himself so that he skimmed. He got the "meat" out of that which he read. I suppose there were days when he went through many more volumes than two. He was learning every day. Therefore, it was no surprise when he stood before an audience and quoted poetry almost endlessly, because he had prepared his mind and his heart. He had the desire. He was consistent in his preparation.

It is in this area of regularity that I would suggest that each of us, as students and learners, be consistent for our future growth and development. This is the only way I know to keep out of that rut.

How Can You Be Consistent?

I learned a few years ago as a struggling student that it isn't so much the time one invests, but rather the regularity of the hours invested. I discovered, for example, that if I could take four hours a day and prepare myself, that was all that was required to keep myself at the head of the class. But it required my studying during the same time every day.

Thus, I discovered what many young people fail to realize. If you are a typical student, you will tend to study when you feel like it. Tomorrow night it might be from six to ten. You might get up early one morning, because it is a crash week, and try from four until eight. You might try it from two to six in the library on another day.

The Mind and the Body

I have found that the mind functions exactly like the physical body. During baseball season I noticed as I went into spring training that I had to be regular in my physical training habits if my body was to perform the way I wanted it to. I noticed that even though I had a good record the year before, I couldn't walk out in April and say, "Look out, crowd, I'm a twenty-game winner!" My body wasn't ready. It had to be developed all over again.

As I went through the very arduous task of performing on the field to get muscles and coordination ready for the opening game, I noticed that it usually required about three weeks to get into condition. Until a ball player invests time regularly every day, he can't produce physically.

Four Hours a Day—Regularly

The mind works like the body—it must be exercised regularly. I promise you that if you will commence a program of study—same time, same station, every day for a maximum of four hours and minimum of two—you will be a scholar in any field that you desire within a two-year period. You will be in the top two percent of all the people with whom you are compared.

After coming back from World War II, I found that I was literally a senior citizen—at least according to the age of most college students. With a wife and two children, I went back to school after five years of professional baseball, at the age of twenty-seven—and to an eighteen-year-old, that is a senior citizen!

There were times when I was brought up rather short. I remember later in my graduate program there was a young girl sitting next to me in one class. I was in my thirties at the time, and she was just a sweet girl of nineteen. We were talking about world civilization—past history—and a campaign in which I had had a part during World War II. (It is fascinating to sit in a history class and realize that you were part of that history!) I thought I would raise my grade by making some wonderful comment—you've had that feeling, haven't you—so I raised my hand and made an observation concerning the point being considered.

Then the young lady leaned over and said, "Were *you* there?"

I said, "Yes, that's right."

She looked at me as if I'd walked off Shiloh Hill in the Civil War!

Well, I found a real challenge in coming back to school after nine years. As a married man trying to care for my family, I was spending eight and ten hours a day at a full-time job and was going to school besides. I was ending up with C's and D's at best—which was quite an improvement over my high school record, but not much for the college standard. Well, before long I became discouraged. (You know how you want to throw in the towel occasionally.)

Finally I went to work applying this little formula of studying the same time every day, and after several months my study time narrowed down to four hours. I noticed that with the same investment of time I could raise my grade from a C to a B and from a B to an A. After maintaining the A level for a period of time, I could commence, because of the training, to reduce the hours from four to three and later from three to about two on most occasions and still maintain the same grade average because I did it every day with regularity.

The Mind Must Be Trained

The mind has to be trained like the body. For the first two weeks of studying at the same hour every day, you won't get any more results than before you tried. But on about the fifteenth day it happens!

Did you ever try to go on a diet? Well, this is another physical phenomenon that sets in at age thirty. When I was playing ball, I couldn't get any heavier than 165 pounds, even with five meals a day and all the malts and pastries in between.

I had a brother six years my senior who was really skinny and quite a bit smaller in stature. Then at age thirty something happened to him. He just—"whifttt"— out he went. I used to rib him—you know how younger brothers will do. I suggested that he get a job with Ringling Brothers and let them mark him "Goodyear" and put him up as a blimp.

Well, he patted me on the head and said, "Go ahead and laugh. One day you are going to be thirty."

"Not I. No, I am 165 pounds and I'll stay this way all my life!"

Then my thirtieth birthday came. They brought in the cake (all the family had gathered) and had me blow out the candles. I did. Then—"whifttt"—I went out too! Shortly after, I went up to 205.

As I got a little older, I finally did like everybody else —I vowed, "I'm going to get on a diet and get back to my playing weight. I want to look like an all-American athlete." I got on a program, but for the first two weeks—nothing! I'd starve myself, I'd exercise, I'd go through more programs than you can imagine, and I'd get on the scale—205! I decided it didn't work. So I quit. But if I had just stayed at it for fifteen days, I would have had results!

That is the way the mind works—the same as the body. This is what will happen if you will try four hours a day (or two hours at a minimum). On the fifteenth day your mind, like your body, will commence to focus and open ready for work. It will be disciplined. For the first fourteen days, if you are typical you will sit down and try to study. You know you have to do it. You are disciplined. You have even moved to an area where study is appropriate. You commence to read. But your mind is everywhere but where it ought to be. It has crawled back to the dance last night. It has gone to watch TV with the group.

How many times have you gone to the refrigerator in four hours? I used to put a note inside the door, "Get back to work!" Well, for fifteen days I applied it, and do you know what happened? On the fifteenth day my mind said, "Okay, Paul, let's go. Back to the book." That was a fascinating discovery. People had told me, but I just hadn't done it. The key is to study the same hours every day without variation.

Understand

Second, when you read and study at the same time every day, do it with purpose and understanding. That's easy to say, isn't it? Now how do you do that? Well, I always have to work the simple way. That is the way my mind has developed.

I have found that certain little gimmicks, methods, techniques (call them what you will) have helped me. May I suggest some. (I experimented with these with some of our missionaries in the field, and it is fascinating to see what they can do.) Did you ever read a chapter and then, after putting the book down, you couldn't tell anybody what you had read? You see, it is easy to read mechanically without understanding. You did the assignment, but got no results. You went through the physical motion, but couldn't recall a thing.

I found that if I could sit down regularly and read with understanding, I couldn't forget. Before reading with understanding, I found that when I picked up a scripture or a textbook and started to read, I just read words but not meaning. Let's take an example. This verse in Alma tells about the great general Moroni and says:

> And Moroni was a strong and a mighty man; he was a man of a perfect understanding; yea, a man that did not delight in bloodshed; a man whose soul did joy in the liberty and freedom of his country, and his brethren from bondage and slavery. (Alma 48:11.)

Now what is the meaning of that verse? At about this point I would turn my book over and ask myself, "What did that passage say?"

So I tried to discipline myself as I read. And by giving myself an accounting orally or in written form, I found that in two or three days I could tell you everything I had read. Then I added another verse and another verse, and after two or three weeks I could read two or three pages and finally chapters and still remember what I had read.

By using simple devices, you cannot forget what you read. After much practice you can even learn to skip over words that are insignificant—prepositions and the little connecting words that make it flow—to where you are reading concepts and principles rather than just words.

I found that if I wanted to sharpen my understanding of a concept or principle, I would set my book aside and call upon my youngest daughter to see if I could explain the point in question to her. If I could teach the principle or idea so that she could understand, then I knew that I knew it. Following that I tried the same experiment on my teenage daughter, upgrading the approach to see if she understood. Then I would bring in my wife and try it out on the adult level. If you can teach a principle at those different levels, you cannot forget it. You may forget what chapter and verse it is in, but you will never forget the principle, the concept, or the idea.

The method doesn't matter. It's the principle that counts—read and study with understanding.

Have a Plan

Too often we begin a course or program without any organized system as to how we hope to accomplish our objective.

How many times have you sat in a congregation where a leader or teacher was challenging you to read the Old Testament, New Testament, or the Book of Mormon? You got all inspired and enthused after hearing his counsel, and then you went home to set up your reading program. You no doubt started with Genesis and after weeks and weeks, if you were diligent, you plowed all the way through to Malachi. The only problem was that you didn't get anything out of it.

I don't know of a quicker way to get discouraged than to try to read the Old Testament from Genesis to Malachi. In fact, if you get through it with any degree of understanding or meaning, you are indeed a rare person, because the book wasn't written to be read in that order. Nor was the New Testament written to be read from Matthew through Revelation. Instead, you need to devise a system or a plan that is workable for you. And there are as many plans as there are students involved.

Here is a plan that has helped me, and I give it merely as an illustration. I find if I am reading the New Testament, that my mind, being as simple as it is, must have an understanding of the whole before the individual books make sense. For me to sit down and commence reading with Matthew and read to the conclusion of Revelation would be foolish because I could never fit it all together. In my great struggle of yesteryear—and it is still going on —I found that if I could just read Luke and Acts together first, as a unit, I got the whole picture of what was going on. Then I could reinforce it by reading Mark, Matthew, and John, in that order. Then I would read 1 Thessalonians, 2 Thessalonians, 1 Corinthians, 2 Corinthians, in that order, and so on, chronologically, through the New Testament as Paul and other writers had contributed to it.

Suggestions for Studying the Scriptures

Following is a list of books from the Old and New Testaments in the order in which they might be read. They are not in chronological order, but by studying them in this manner, the reader will get an overview of the whole. The individual books and letters will then have far greater meaning.

Old Testament

Genesis
Exodus
Leviticus (*chapters 8, 9, 10, and 17*)
Numbers
Deuteronomy (*chapters 4, 14, 27, and 30*)
Joshua
Judges
Ruth
1 Samuel
2 Samuel
Omit 1 and 2 Kings (*first time through*)
Omit 1 and 2 Chronicles (*first time through*)

Amos
Hosea
Isaiah
Jeremiah
Ezekiel
Minor Prophets (*Obadiah, Jonah, etc.*)
Job
Psalms
Proverbs
Omit Song of Solomon and Ecclesiastes (*first time through*)

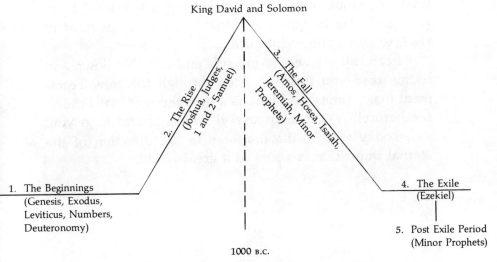

King David and Solomon

2. The Rise
(Joshua, Judges,
1 and 2 Samuel)

3. The Fall
(Amos, Hosea, Isaiah,
Jeremiah, Minor
Prophets)

1. The Beginnings
(Genesis, Exodus,
Leviticus, Numbers,
Deuteronomy)

4. The Exile
(Ezekiel)

5. Post Exile Period
(Minor Prophets)

1000 B.C.

New Testament

Luke-Acts
Mark
Matthew
John
1 Thessalonians }
2 Thessalonians } 2nd Journey
1 Corinthians ⎫
2 Corinthians ⎬ 3rd Journey
Galatians ⎪
Romans ⎭
Colossians ⎫
Ephesians ⎬ 4th Journey
Philemon ⎪ 1st Roman
Philippians ⎭   imprisonment

Hebrews ⎫
1 Timothy ⎬ Freed from prison—but
Titus ⎭   in Rome
2 Timothy ⎫
James ⎬ 2nd Roman imprisonment
1 and 2 Peter
1, 2, and 3 John
Jude
Revelation

I have done the same with all the scriptures. The important thing is having a purpose and a plan and knowing where you are going and how you intend to get there and then doing it with regularity, meaning, and understanding.

Learning Is Delightful

Learning is one of the most delightful of all the activities that our Heavenly Father has given us in our mortal lives. It is an on-going process. Where I used to sit and think, "Oh, will I be glad when this year is over! I'm tired of school. Why did I get *him* for a teacher?" I can now go home tonight and think, "Can I get an hour to read, to study the scriptures?"

I can call my wife to my side and say, "Sit down and let me read you this. I've been through the New Testament many times, and here is a new thought that I didn't see before!" What a discovery! I recommend it to you.

Today will be the first step in the direction of the eternal quest that is yours in a great world.

CHAPTER 4

Blessed Are the Teachable

Latter-day Saint on Assignment

I was leaving my home in Downey, California, one evening to attend to an assignment out in the San Fernando Valley. In California we normally have to take into account the traffic conditions, particularly on the Sabbath. I allowed myself a good hour and a half, but on this occasion it was not quite enough. Seeing that I was running about ten minutes late, I took what I thought was an excellent shortcut. That was my first mistake.

The freeway system down there changes almost weekly, and the ramp that was to put me on the shortcut route had become kind of a dead-end street with a neatly placed sign that read, "No left turn." Now that is exactly where I had to go. Well, this proved to be my second mistake. The traffic was not very heavy, and as I got to the end of the ramp, I looked to the right and to the left and, finding no traffic, I made the turn.

I felt terrible, particularly because it was the Sabbath and it was not right in the first place. I felt very guilty. Then I looked in the rear view mirror and found out why. Coming right behind me was the Highway Patrol. I do not know where he came from, because it was completely clear just a moment before. He had that flashing red light blinking, which signaled me to pull over, and so I did.

I sat there and wound down the window, waiting for the inevitable meeting. As he got out of the squad car, he looked, from where I was sitting, to be about seven feet three inches tall. I never saw so much authority in a man in all my life!

He came over to the side of the car looking very stern, but he was quite polite. He leaned down and said, "What's your hurry, buddy?"

I said, "This is a terrible thing to have to admit, but I knew I was wrong when I turned. I saw the sign. Your being a man of the law, I know you'll want to have all the facts. I'm going to church." And I thought that would make all the difference in the world.

He didn't even bat an eye. He reached into his back pocket and pulled out his ticket book. He flipped open the cover and was almost ready to write when I interrupted again, saying, "Now wait just a minute. You have to have all the facts before you decide that I am guilty. Before you make your final judgment, let me tell you something else. Not only am I going to church, but I'm on the program. There are over 300 people waiting to hear me tonight. Doesn't that make a difference in my case?"

He started to write, showing no compassion whatsoever. So I came back with still a third plea, reminding him that these were dedicated people who were anxiously awaiting the word of the Lord. I said, "Doesn't the objective of my trip suggest mercy in this case?"

Then for the first time he looked up and said, kind of gruffly, "What church are you going to?"

I said, "I'm a Latter-day Saint, and I'm ten minutes late right now! Does that help?"

He said, "You know, that makes a great deal of difference. I'm a high councilman. Get on your way!"

I want to tell you that I learned that it pays to keep the gospel light out from under the bushel. Rest assured that I did repent and promised myself that my future objective would always be to set a proper example.

There are lots of fringe benefits in this Church. In fact, I went home later and reported this true incident to my good family. One daughter is rather artistically inclined, and without any prompting from me, she quietly tiptoed out of the room. She reappeared about fifteen minutes later with a little sign that she had printed. It said simply in gold leaf, "LATTER-DAY SAINT ON ASSIGNMENT." Now when I get into one of those questionable situations, as I occasionally do—like when I hit a yellow light and don't know whether to go or stop—I just hold up the sign as I go through.

Counting the Cost

The Department of Education provides some very excellent Church facilities at the various colleges and universities. We have a number of such institute buildings in the south land. I used the institute of religion building at the University of Southern California for an office. This required that I travel frequently—in fact, daily—from my home in Downey to the USC campus and back.

I am the type of fellow who gets very concerned about being in a rut. I like a change of environment, new things, challenges. So quite frequently I would take a different road to work just to break the monotony. I disliked driving on the freeway, looking at all those license plates day after day.

One morning as I made a tour through the northern part of our fair city, I went down a street that I had not traveled before. Lo and behold, I noticed under construction one of the finest looking houses I had ever seen! This house struck my fancy because it was almost identical to a plan that my wife had hoped we would one day build.

I found myself, more often than not, going that way just to see the progress on the house that was not even mine. (I am sure everyone does things like this in their own way.) A month or two went by and the house was about two-thirds completed. Then one morning as I passed that way, I noticed that the workmen had ceased their labors. No work was being accomplished.

The days grew into weeks. The thing that gave me the most concern, as I am sure it did the owner, was that the once bright, shiny, new lumber was now starting to fade because it was not yet painted. It turned first to a light brown, then to a darker brown, and then to a kind of off-yellow, indicating that the deterioration process had set in. As I made one of my frequent trips by that way, I thought how unfortunate it was that more insight and vision had not gone into the planning.

Then one morning as I passed by to see if there had been any progress, one of the eternal truths of the New Testament came very forcefully to my mind as I viewed the situation. Luke tells about an incident in the life of the Savior when a great multitude gathered and, as they frequently did, commenced to ask questions in an attempt to trap Him. In this particular setting the Savior made a very profound observation, so profound that it is just as applicable here today as it was in the time in which He uttered it.

He said, as He turned to meet the multitude:

For which of you, intending to build a tower, sitteth not down first, and counteth the cost, whether he have sufficient to finish it?

Lest haply, after he hath laid the foundation, and is not able to finish it, all that behold it begin to mock him,

Saying this man began to build, and was not able to finish.

[Then He went on to suggest another possibility]:

Or what king, going to make war against another king, sitteth not down first, and consulteth whether he be able with ten thousand to meet him that cometh against him with twenty thousand? (Luke 14:28-31.)

Now this logic makes pretty good sense, doesn't it? Some of us who were in World War II or the Korean conflict remember many occasions when we would receive orders to push out and take a certain pillbox, or a given military objective, that the enemy occupied. The first thing we always did as infantrymen was to sit and consider the odds. How strong was our force? How heavy was the firepower? Each time we found ourselves outnumbered in one of these categories, we very politely sat still until we gained reinforcements or additional strength. One of the reasons I am here today is that we applied that logic.

Isn't it interesting, though, that as true and valid as that idea is, few people ever follow its wisdom? We can sometimes see it in immediate relationships, but not always in the eternal scheme.

Maybe we could make application to the tower the Savior refers to as it might apply to eternal life. We can say, in essence, "For which of us, intending to build eternal lives, sitteth not down first and consulteth whether we will have sufficient to complete the task?"

The process of educating the body, the mind, and the spirit is the foundation on which this can be achieved. That is why it is a thrill to see groups of Latter-day Saints assemble to seek to further the educational process. Too few people today take the time to add to their "eternal" foundation by seeking knowledge through learning.

I was impressed as I was doing some reading a number of months ago when I came across some observations made by much greater minds than mine relative to this whole process of keeping our minds open and fertile at all times. Let me share a few of my favorites with you.

One educator says, "Some people grow with responsibility; others just swell."

Will Rogers, that great actor-comedian-philosopher, made a very succinct statement early in his life. He said, "Everyone is ignorant, only on different subjects."

Disraeli put it this way: "Every man has a right to be conceited until he is successful."

Francis Bacon reminds us that the less people speak of their greatness, the more others will think of it.

Vincent Massey, the former premier of Canada, said it in still another way: "A highbrow is one whose learning has outstripped his intelligence."

Tennyson said, "True humility is the highest virtue —mother of them all."

Edgar Jones, not too many years ago, told a great audience that among all of the great men whom he had ever know or watched during his lifetime, none had been without humility, restraint, or deliberation.

I think those are profound thoughts. While they are very idealistic in nature, they suggest to me the great process by which we can come not only to know ourselves more completely, but what we must do to make the proper application.

My father-in-law was not a member of this Church. He was a great Protestant minister. I suppose if there were a counterpart of an apostle in the Disciple of Christ organization, this would have been his position. He was termed "Minister-at-Large," and he was called all over the world to represent this great body of individuals.

He was at one time the president of a university

sponsored by their church. He later became the head of
Brite Bible College at Texas Christian University, which
would be their counterpart to BYU. In this position he
frequently entertained correspondence from would-be
faculty members.

Shortly after his death, as I was helping my wife and
her good mother sort out some of his materials, I came
across a very interesting letter that was addressed to him
by a member seeking a position on his faculty. It said:

My Dear Sir:

*Notified May 21 that financial stress let me out here
without disgrace because I was a latecomer on the faculty.
I teach almost anything in modern French, German, and
Spanish—language, literature, courses for teaching, scientific material, and phonetics. I have made thirty-one public
addresses since last January 1st. I have taught in three
high schools, one state teachers' college, two state universities, and three denominational colleges. War, pestilence,
and famine—not inefficiency—make changes necessary.*

*Keep sane by hobby of music, by playing the flute, bari-
tone bass, alto horn, clarinet, and cello. Can direct and
lead choruses, bands, or orchestras, including the a cap-
pella choir which is now so popular. Have taught the cello
for years and can instruct in all band instruments. Keep
well by physical education. Have long taught and can still
instruct, as a side line, in corrective exercises, floor activities, and gymnasium, line apparatus, heavy German
gymnastics, and swimming.*

*Health lecturer. Used repeatedly for institute work in
this capacity. I prefer teaching to research, though I keep
up advanced studies. Taught high school administration
during seven summer sessions. Teacher of German this
summer for the third time.*

*Your correspondence invited. Scholastic record en-
closed.*

Respectfully yours,

If you sat in the position of my father-in-law and had to make the decision as to whether you would include this man on your faculty, what would you do? If a like individual in your particular Church organization seemingly radiated this kind of egotism, would you be inclined to want to include him or her in the program?

I do not mean to suggest that we should not be self-confident in letting people know our abilities and talents, but here is a man who suggests by his attitude that he has learned it all! "There is nothing I don't know! You would be most fortunate to include me in your organization." Chances are each of us would look very seriously for the individual who still had an attitude of wanting to learn more and one who would listen to the other fellow.

Knowing Too Much

I have noticed that this has become one of the real problems that we face in society, business, and industry. I spoke to a group of bank executives in southern California, and one of them brought to my attention a report that I think is interesting. He told of some one hundred employees whom they had just taken into the organization and sent back East for one year's training. He said, "Brother Dunn, the interesting thing is that within six months, although they were all college graduates and capable men in their fields, 90 percent of them failed."

I wanted to know why. His comment surprised me a great deal. He simply said, "They know too much." In other words, their minds are closed to other possibilities in the learning process. They had literally gone into the field to tell their boss how to run the organization and had failed to learn this one great principle of life taught so capably by the Savior: "Blessed are the meek: for they shall [literally] inherit the earth." (Matthew 5:5.) This is exactly what the Savior taught, through example and word, to all mankind.

Blessed Are the Open-minded

I was quite interested in what Bruce Barton said a number of years ago in this connection: "The biggest problem that we have is in getting people to change, to move from one level to another. When we are through changing, we are through." There is a lot in what he says, particularly in how he says it.

The biggest men have remained open-minded to the end. I do not need to recall to your attention the contribution of Benjamin Franklin. As a man in his eightieth year, he was still seeking earnestly for new truths and ways of improving mankind and his environment.

President David O. McKay taught me more of what an open-minded person should be like than I had ever learned in twelve years of college education because of his alert, sensitive mind and his ability to progress within himself.

I have long appreciated what the Savior suggested to us by way of being meek and open-minded. Let me paraphrase a little more completely what I feel the Savior might have intended as He spoke this one truth in that great Sermon on the Mount: "Blessed are the meek." Perhaps He might say today before a similar group, "Blessed are those of us who are open-minded, who keep our energies properly focused, aiming always upward and onward. Blessed are those of us who are still teachable and can change from what we are to something still better." There we have in a nutshell the answer to eternal progression.

Cult of Mediocrity

If there is one fear that I have as I look at the average Latter-day Saint, it is the tendency on the part of many to become somewhat complacent or to feel that they have attained all they need. Quite frequently as I instruct adult groups, I get the feeling that, rather than have me suggest other possibilities or tap some new insights in the principle being considered, they would much prefer that I merely restate in other terms what they already believe, that I give them reassurance of the testimony that is already theirs. Too frequently people in our own Church want entertainment rather than education.

I was intensely interested in what Herbert Hoover said about this. He said, "The great danger facing the American people is the possibility of our developing a cult of mediocre individuals." He went on to point out the paradox that exists. He said, "Isn't it interesting that when you think of yourself, you never think of the average person." We are always above average in our own evaluation.

When I was a teenager in school, I used to think about replacing Bob Feller and a few others. I never thought of myself as just a "C" league ballplayer. I was always beating Bob Feller and striking out Lou Gehrig and Babe Ruth! I had the greatest visions you could ever imagine in this connection. We all do. And this is good.

But Hoover said that the interesting thing is that in thinking of ourselves as above average, few of us want to pay the price to become uncommon. We want to be better than average, but we do not want to invest the time or energy or develop the ability to achieve it. He said it this way: "It's amazing when you become ill that you do not want an average doctor. You want the best."

When your car goes on the blink, you don't want Brother Dunn to fix it. (This is very obvious if you know my mechanical skills!) I had a car go out on me and took it in for repairs. Unfortunately I got a common mechanic, and it cost me an extra $50. I too want the most skilled individual I can find to work on my car.

Hoover took it a step further. He said, "When you get into trouble, you seek the most skilled lawyer who can be found. When you go into battle, isn't it amazing that you want the most capable admirals and generals leading your army and navy, not the average run-of-the-mill."

This is a challenge to every Latter-day Saint. Our Church statistics indicate that about 60 percent, or the majority, are willing to settle for the average. It is the minority that will step out to change the picture.

Example of Meekness

Let me share with you some of the great ideas that I have long appreciated in my study of the Old and the New Testaments, particularly, and in life, generally. Moses, you recall, was the great leader of the Hebrew people. On many occasions he showed his mortal and weak side, yet because of his strong mind and will, and with the aid of the Lord, it is recorded in Numbers: "Now the man Moses was very meek, above all the men which were upon the face of the earth." (12:3.)

As I read between the lines, he was great because he had a *teachable mind.* He was willing to change whenever change was necessary.

Jeremiah, that courageous, brilliant statesman in the era of the prophets, had this recorded of him, "Then said I, Ah, Lord God! Behold, I cannot speak: for I am a child." (Jeremiah 1:6.)

He gained confidence not from recognized power on his own, but from the conviction that the Lord Jehovah had said to him, "For thou shalt go to all that I shall send

thee, and whatsoever I command thee thou shalt speak."
(Jeremiah 1:7.) He had to achieve this through an open,
teachable mind.

Paul, one of the most outstanding of all the apostles,
was highly educated and proud of his Roman citizenship.
Yet he speaks of himself as a weak specimen of humanity
and the greatest of all sinners, so humble and concerned
was he for his own growth.

Sir Isaac Newton, discoverer of the law of gravity,
declared in sweet humility:

> I do not know what I may appear to the world; but to
> myself I seem to have been only a boy playing by the sea-
> shore and diverting myself in now and then finding a
> smoother pebble or a prettier shell than ordinary, while
> the great ocean of truth lay undiscovered before me.

That great emancipator Abraham Lincoln frankly
admitted to his critics that he might be the very fool of
whom they spoke, particularly when they criticized him
for putting in his cabinet individuals who appeared on the
surface to be more capable than he. "If I found more like
them I would staff my cabinet," he answered, for he had a
teachable spirit, willing always to learn from the other
fellow.

The list is long, and I think the Savior summed it up
most admirably when He said, "Blessed are the meek"—
the teachable, those of us who will remain open-minded to
the end. We are not only the ones who will inherit the
earth, but we will continue to progress forever and ever,
because education is an eternal process.

A Salute

While serving as director at the University of Southern California in our institute program, I had an oppor-

tunity to accept an assignment offered by that school to represent the Church among many educators and religious leaders. There were some 2,000 people who assembled at this particular education conference to discuss and learn ways and means of curbing some of the problems that face our young people today. Most of us were new to each other, and we were from all parts of the country.

The president of the university, being the genial host that he was, provided a very fine luncheon just prior to our conference presentations. I noticed as I stepped into the dining area that I had been placed right beside a man in full navy uniform, a commander by rank. As we took our places, which were identified by little place cards, he turned to me and said, "Mr. Dunn, I would like to get acquainted with you." We shook hands and he said, "You're a Latter-day Saint, aren't you?"

I thought, "Good heavens! What have I done to tip my hand already?" And I said, "Yes, how did you know?"

He said, "I noticed that you are not going to partake of that liquid." There was the clue: I had turned my cup over. As we frequently do almost mechanically, I started to defend my position.

He interrupted me very quickly and said, "Look, I didn't inquire about your background to get a defense of your position."

I then asked him why, and he said, "I wanted to take this opportunity to salute you, sir. May I?"

Now I was only a Pfc in World War II. Any time a Navy commander wants to salute a private, I am not going to stop him. So I turned to him and said, "Yes, sir. Please go ahead."

Then he kind of hurt my ego a little. He said, "Well, I don't mean you personally. I mean the organization that you are representing today—the great Latter-day Saint faith."

I was very inquisitive. I wanted to know why he had singled us out. As we sat down, I inquired. I said, "Why do you pay tribute to my Church?"

He said, "Very simple. In my assignment as a Navy commander, I am in charge of the testing program for the United States Navy. But even prior to this I had an opportunity to travel all over the world. I have watched your people with keen interest."

He was a sharp, capable leader himself, and he continued, "Mr. Dunn, I don't know what it is about you people, but you have something that gets through to me. It's an air of confidence; it's an ideal; it's something that I can't quite put my hands on. But I'm convinced, sir, that one day this country—in fact, this world—will look to you people for spiritual direction.

"I want to take this opportunity as a family man, as an educator, and as a member of the armed forces to salute you, sir, and your Church for your wonderful standards and spiritual truths. It gives us all a sense of well-being just to know that such an organization exists."

Can you appreciate a little how proud I felt inside because individuals of this caliber know what we are? I thought as he gave us this tribute, "What a responsibility we each have not only to measure up, but to assume adequately the positions that our Heavenly Father has placed upon us to go and assist the world in literally becoming the kingdom of God."

We can do this not only by teaching the revelations that have come, but by continuing the educational process. We become the tools and the instruments in the hands of the Lord. We will not only achieve the goal the Lord has set, but we will continue to build the tower (eternal lives), because we sat first and considered the cost and through the learning process accomplished it.

CHAPTER 5

Be Not Ashamed

I recall a fascinating young man named George, a recent convert in the New England Mission, who had a very interesting life and story. The missionaries found him shortly after he was released from Walpole Prison in Massachusetts. George was a wonderful contact. I will not divulge all of his background, but here are George's own words as he tells how he came in contact with the elders and what the impact was then and now in his life since joining the Church.

Well, I was at my sister's wedding. I had met this young girl who happened to be a student at BYU, and I asked her out for a date. On a few occasions she had mentioned the Church. But on this date she said to me that her religion meant more to her than anything and everything. When she said that to me, it really stuck in my mind and had a great effect. The next day I called up the mission home, and I spoke to President Dunn's wife and asked if I could find out a little bit more about the Church. She took my name and address and said that she would send the elders out to visit me.

I said that would be fine and I would be available. The following day I was looking forward to these old fel-

lows with long white beards and the big hats, and, to my amazement, these two clean-cut fellows with short hair and three-button suits with vests came up the stairs and started talking to me about the Church. Then I just took the lessons from there. It was shortly after that when I was baptized.

I asked, "George, without any attempt to embarrass you, could you tell us the kind of life you came from and what the gospel has meant in the change?"

Well, I lived what some people might describe as a rather colorful life. In my particular calling I was called by Satan. Through my early years I did not have opportunities as some Latter-day Saints have. I was brought up in the type of environment where I had to reach out and get the things I wanted, and the things that I wanted were material things. So slowly, as I grew older, I progressed and became more efficient in my profession. I started breaking into homes and business establishments until I learned how to open safes. I was in the environment with a lot of people with colorful pasts.

Since the gospel has come into my life, it has just changed me 100 percent. I spent most of my time in nightclubs and cabarets and in fancy cars with people who always were trying to see how much they could take in life. And since I have been in this Church, it has been just reversed. I have just realized there are so many greater things in life than the type of life that I was living before I came into the Church.

Finally, I asked him if he could bear his testimony and tell us how he feels inside now.

Well, I am grateful for this opportunity. I am thankful for my membership in this Church, and I hope that I can be accepted and get a chance to know everyone on a little more personal basis. I came here from Boston, Mas-

*sachusetts, to let you know that I have a testimony of the
gospel. I hope that maybe some of you might be able to catch
the message as I bear you my witness. I know that there is
a prophet who walks on this earth today, as in olden days.
I know that God lives and that He loves each and every
one of you here today. I know, without a shadow of a
doubt, that Jesus is the Christ and that He lives. And although I have spent my days in prison, if you do not know
that the gospel is true, then you too are prisoners. And
until that day comes when you free yourselves, you will
remain as I was, a prisoner. I bear you my witness in the
name of Jesus Christ.*

I think we see in George and many like him the qual-
ities of one who is not ashamed of the gospel of Jesus
Christ. I have had a chance to come to know this young
man quite intimately, and I can testify that his life before
the Lord is now clean and wholesome and wonderful.
And that is what this Church is all about. I hope that you
will never be afraid or ashamed of the gospel of Jesus
Christ.

Be Identified

As you perhaps know, Harmon Killebrew plays baseball for the Minnesota Twins ball club, and Brother Killebrew is not ashamed of the gospel of Jesus Christ. He is a
quiet, silent, wonderful miracle worker.

He called me on the phone one evening and said,
"Paul, would it be possible in your schedule to come
down Sunday morning and talk to the Minnesota Twins
ball club?"

I said, "I'd be honored, Harmon. What can I do?"

He said, "Just teach them the gospel of Jesus Christ,
but don't tell them you are doing it."

And I said, "Well, how did you get this program arranged?"

Then this great athlete said, "I'm the program chair-
man for our devotional services."

I said, "I didn't know ball clubs had devotional services."

He said, "The Minnesota Twins do, and I'm it."

So I went down to the Statler-Hilton there in Boston
one Sunday morning, and there assembled before me
were many Minnesota Twin ball players and their wives.

There in an upper room in a quiet, peaceful, reverent
manner we talked, not about baseball, although that entered in a time or two, but about eternal verities that really
change lives—goals and aspirations in our lives. All this
happened because Harmon Killebrew was not ashamed to
be identified.

Billy Casper came to town for the great Avco Classic.
He wanted to know if we could get together about some
missionary business. I was honored and went out as his
special guest to the country club.

Because he had shot the worst round in his professional career on that very course one year before, he came
back for revenge. (That year he won that classic by a
stroke or two.) During that great event staged at Sut-
ton, Massachusetts, he invited me to be his spiritual
caddy.

As we came back into the clubhouse after a practice
round, I tried to beg off and say, "Well, now, I'd better
leave you alone."

"No, you come in here," he replied as the reporters
mobbed him.

We got back in a private section of the clubhouse
where the big stars were lockered, and every reporter
from any major newspaper in Massachusetts had him sur-
rounded. You know what they wanted to talk about? Golf,
golf, golf.

But Billy is not ashamed of who he is or what he

represents. So he said, "No, we're not going to talk about golf right now. I've brought another man, and he's going to talk to you." Pointing to me, he said, "This is President Dunn of the New England Mission."

"Well, what's that?" they asked.

"He's going to talk to you about it."

So for a few moments we sat in the seclusion of the clubhouse and talked about things that matter most, and the reporters were fascinated. For the first ten minutes, they tried to get back to golf, but Billy said, "Now if you want an interview, listen." So they listened while he told them about the gospel and the Church.

Meeting the Cardinal

When I first arrived in New England, I received a call from a Catholic father at Boston College, one of the great institutions in the East. We chatted about the niceties of the great area to which we were both assigned, and finally he said, "Dr. Dunn, would you come over and tell us about your faith?"

I said, "Thank you for the honor. If I might speak very frankly, I don't know that you want me under the conditions that I am committed to come."

"Why is that?" he said.

"I have been sent here by a prophet of the Lord to warn all people that the gospel has been restored, and I would naturally have to teach that concept.

"I've worked for our Church on many campuses throughout the country, and I know that probably very little good will come from my visit other than the fact that you'll be more convinced that you're right and I'll go home convinced that I'm right. I have been sent here for three years to call all people to repentance."

"Thank you for your honesty," he answered, and he hung up.

Six weeks later he called again. "This is Father _____. Do you remember?"

"Yes, I remember our conversation," I said.

"I'd like to have you come and talk to my class," he remarked. "We have many who will be ordained to the ministry shortly."

I said, "Do you remember the circumstances under which I would come?"

"Yes," he said. "We'd like to have you on that basis."

I said, "Fine, I'm your man." And so I took two elders and went over.

While there I met the distinguished cardinal of New England, and he was a very fascinating giant of a man in his own right. He was not known to smile very much, however, and I thought, "Here is the supreme test."

When we were introduced, I was presented to him as the head of the Mormon Church in the New England area. So I tried to qualify that.

I said, "No, sir, I'm really a cardinal myself."

He said, "You are?"

I said, "Yes, sir."

He said, "I didn't think they had the position of cardinal in the Mormon Church."

I said, "They don't. I played for St. Louis." Well, he almost smiled.

When we were presented to the class, they looked interested, and I had my two assistants stand and speak for about five minutes each. I don't think the importance of what they said was quite as great as what they radiated. They were twenty-one-year-old boys who had left their home to preach the gospel of Jesus Christ. Their spirit and testimony was evident.

As my first assistant started to speak, the first ciga-

rette went out and then the second. The audience started
to sit more erect in their tablet armchairs, and they listened
very attentively. The second assistant told of Joseph
Smith's vision in such a manner that a real spiritual feeling
was experienced by all present.

Then it came my turn, and after visiting with them for
a few moments and trying to create a proper rapport, I
took from my pocket the thirteen Articles of Faith and
read each one in turn, giving a little two-minute dissertation on each. I concluded by bearing solemn witness and
testimony of this Church. Then it happened—almost as if
a baton in the hand of a choir director had been set up as
a signal, the class arose in unison and for about a minute
gave three Mormon elders a standing ovation.

We found out why a little later. One by one, as they
approached the front of the room, taking each one of us
by the hand, the comment was, "Thank God there are
some people in the world who won't compromise."

And out of that experience came great teaching
moments. Now that is the kind of an image and impact
you can have on people of the world if you are not
ashamed of the gospel of Jesus Christ.

Standing Up to Be Counted

Some years ago I served this great country as a
World War II soldier. I am proud that I had the opportunity to serve, because I love this country and what it
represents. I would do it again and again.

I know what it is for a country and a people to lose
their freedom. I know what a prison camp is. I know what
happens when minds are directed to think only one
philosophy.

I had the opportunity while on the island of Guam as
a soldier in World War II to enter a concentration camp

that had incarcerated many thousands of people for three years. I saw a Baptist minister in that camp who, although six feet tall, weighed only seventy pounds. He struggled through the mud and tugged my boot and thanked me as an American liberator, because I represented freedom. Do you know what his first request was? Tears in his eyes, lying there in the mud, he asked, "Soldier, do you have an American flag?"

"No, sir," I replied, "but I can get one."

I got one, and that man, so grateful for his freedom, took that flag and held it to his bosom and just cried. I know a little bit about such things because I was there.

I also know a little bit about the challenge of standing up to be counted as a missionary while in the service. It is not easy. It never was intended to be. One reason we came to this world was to learn, to grow, to progress, to develop.

I got shipped back East as a young inductee, and I ended up in the 77th infantry division. I had such a high IQ that they handed me a rifle and a shovel. That is why young people need all the education they can get. We need qualified people in key positions of leadership. Anybody can dig, but not everybody can think. We need thinkers. We need example setters, pace setters.

The Pfc and the Sergeant

I was put in a company that was really a company. There has not been one to match it. The non-commissioned officer in charge had a sad reputation indeed. (Let me put it this way: In the council in heaven two-thirds followed the Savior and one-third went with another force. I do not know how this man got out. He should have gone with the other third. He was of that element.) He could not speak three words without profaning two. His every thought was of liquor and lust.

He followed the general philosophy that we see in the world today—eat, drink, and be merry, for tomorrow we die. In other words, "Get it now, kids, while you can, because if you don't, you won't live to enjoy it." That was ancient Lamanite philosophy; that was Roman philosophy. It still exists, I notice, on college campuses and in military organizations. It is Satan's finest tool: "Tomorrow is uncertain so grab now!" "When in Rome, do as the Romans do—whatever that is."

My sergeant was always supporting such a philosophy. He and I did not hit it off from the day I walked into the orderly room. Did you ever run into anybody whom you just disliked from the first glance? I hope that does not happen, but it did with the two of us. I thought, "This will be interesting. He has the rank and I have to work under him, and I can pretty well tell he is going to win." And it seemed for a time he did. I continually was on guard and KP.

About two months later we were shipped over to Hawaii, and when we got to Honolulu, things really started to happen. Down on Beretania Street were some houses of ill repute. My sergeant thought that to be a man you had to go down there and participate. He ordered his platoon of thirty to load up one Saturday afternoon when we got our passes, and we were counseled to really have a fling for the weekend. He said that nobody was going to qualify in his platoon until they had had an experience. To him, that was being a man.

I did not know that to be a man was to degrade yourself. I did not know it was to be a man to fall into slavery, to be a servant to the passions of one's emotions. But that was his standard.

Two of us decided to stand up against him. We caught all sorts of dirty detail as a result. He was angry and could not legally do anything about it, but under cover he did quite a bit. We went at this for month after month.

One night I woke up and he was strapping me to my cot. He had two other bullies with him, and they thought they would get a Mormon to share a fifth of whiskey. I got that liquid poured on me from top to bottom, but he could not make me drink it. And that excited him all the more. The challenge was even greater. Well, that was the kind of life we were experiencing.

A Frog Story

One night in combat on the island of Guam we had our perimeters dug. I don't know how they fought in Vietnam, but we used to rally like the pioneers of old and get in a big circle, digging in our foxholes. They always put the privates on the outer perimeter, where the enemy encountered us at night. The higher the rank, the closer to the center you got, which makes sense, of course, if you are trying to save the brass. But I was just a private, so I was stuck out on the outer perimeter. That night it was raining cats and dogs. I was sick with dingue fever and some other problems that went with it, and I thought, "Oh, death, where is thy sting."

Suddenly the enemy opened up with a banzai attack. About that time a grenade came through the trees, and I was lying prone in the hole just below, literally covered with water.

Suddenly something dropped, plop, on my chest. "Well," I thought, "I've got three seconds to find where it landed." Sick, worried, and miserable as I was, I threw off that poncho and tried to locate the grenade. I could not, so I just plugged my ears. It did not go off, so I thought, "Well, my time has not yet come!"

All of a sudden from that mucky hole jumped one of those great, gigantic Guam bullfrogs. Barrup! Just as one of the grenades had gone through a tree, that frog jumped on my chest. Well, how would you feel if you had just gotten your life back again?

As I lay there, I thought, "Well, now, if that worried me that much, what would it do for my sergeant?" So I grabbed the frog. Sergeant Izzo had dug in about ten paces behind me—and we had a policy in World War II that when there was a grenade or a live piece of ammunition in a hole, we would holler, "Fire in the hole." That meant that you had better get out.

As one of the flares went up, I could see Izzo all hunched over with his poncho in the rain. He was reasonably secure in the inner circle. I got up on my knees and thought, "If I could ever throw a strike, I'd like to throw one tonight." So I took that big old frog, and when the next flare was set off, I wound up and threw that frog with all the strength I had.

I hit Izzo right in the head. As I did I hollered, "Fire in the hole." You have never seen a man move like that in your life. I knew what he was going through.

The next morning at breakfast he told us a fantastic war story. He said, "You know what I went through last night?"

"No, Izzo," we answered, "what did you go through last night?"

"One of those grenades landed in my hole. One of you characters is getting too careless."

"Ah," I said, "it sounds like a frog story to me."

Home Again

Out of the one thousand men in the second battalion of the 305th regiment that started in San Francisco, only six of us made it to the end of the war. And you know my luck. I was grateful to be one of the six, but so was Izzo. That man was so mean and so miserable, he seemed indestructible. I believe that of all the spirits that have ever been born, this man had to be one of the most challenging. He was that kind of a person—always in or near the gutter.

The war finally ended, and it was time to rotate the troops home. We were up in a little village called Asahigawa, Japan, and to rotate soldiers home fairly, we were put on a point system. So many points were given for each month spent in the service, so many points for each campaign, so many points for each wound, and so on. The morning they listed the rotation home was one of the greatest days of my life. I walked to the bulletin board, and I led the list. Paul H. Dunn, eighty-seven points, and under me was staff sergeant, Harry Izzo, eighty-five. I just gloated all over.

The night before I was to leave Asahigawa, they threw a party for me in an old Japanese barracks. We pooled our cookies and goodies from home.

About halfway through, Izzo got up and said, "Men, give me your attention." He said, "I use the term men loosely, you are not men. You do not know what life is yet." (The men were recent additions from the States.)

And he went on to use some interesting adjectives that told them what he thought. Then he said, "Tomorrow we're going to let this guy (pointing to me) go home. I'd like to say something about him before he goes.

"When Dunn walked into the orderly room back at Camp Pickett, Virginia, two and a half years ago, we did not like each other. I don't know whether he knows this or not, but I did not like him."

He added, "You know why? Because he represented something I am not, and I felt uncomfortable. I vowed that day that I would do everything in my power to put him in the gutter, but he would not come. We battled for two and a half years. Now tomorrow he goes home."

And he said, "Young men, if I could go home to my wife and family tomorrow with his record, I would give my life."

And here I did not think he had a spark of the divine in him. Well, there were some tears and some goodbyes, and the next day I left and went home to live happily ever after.

Transforming Power

I think about seven years came and went, and then a knock came at my door one evening out in California. I answered the door, and I could not believe it. I thought I was having a revelation.

There in the framework was Harry Izzo. For a minute I thought World War III had started. I did not know whether to let him in or not. I did not want to contaminate my home. I was obviously speechless.

He said, "Do you remember me? (Did I ever!) My wife is out in the car," he continued. "May we come in?"

We invited them in.

"Guess you are wondering what brings us to California."

"Yes, I had thought about it."

"You remember when you left Asahigawa that December morning back in 1945?" he asked.

"Yes, I remember!"

He said, "I went home to Pennsylvania. I was living a good life, and one day two young men knocked on my door. You know who they were?"

"I have an idea," I answered.

He said, "You know, Paul, the only reason I let them in?"

"Why?"

"Because of you. And we listened, and six months later we joined the Church. And we are out here now, and we wondered tonight if you knew that we had joined the Church."

We did not know.

And then he asked us a favor, "Would you do us the honor of standing as a witness in the holy temple as we join hands to become husband and wife forever and have our lovely children sealed to us?"

Well, that is what the gospel does. I have seen men come out of the gutter—filthy, miserable, and no good by any standard. I have seen them finally come to a holy altar after total repentance, a son and child of God. That is the transforming power that you and I experience every day in the Church.

My prayer is that we will hold fast to the things that we learn in the gospel and that we recommit ourselves to the things we know are eternal.

Be not ashamed of the gospel. When you get isolated, as you occasionally do; when you get a little lonesome, as you occasionally do; when you get discouraged, as you occasionally do—just remember there are those who really know that God lives, that Jesus is the Christ.

CHAPTER 6

Keys to Successful Living

A Visitor and a Test

I have a chance to test the youth of the Church occasionally. Not too long ago we had a young man call at my home, pursuing in the way young men will the company of my daughter. On this occasion, the young man rang the doorbell (this was his first date with my daughter), and as I opened the door, he just went limp. You could see his thoughts come to the surface. He seemed to be thinking, "Of all the days you could be home, you *would* pick this one!"

So I invited him in and escorted him into the front room. He stood there nervously awaiting the arrival of my daughter from another room—and hoping every minute that it would be soon.

I asked him to be seated, and then I said, "You don't mind if I visit with you for a moment, do you?"

"No," he answered politely, but you could just see him thinking, "Come on, young lady, make it quick!"

We chatted, and I got acquainted with a little of his history and background. For a moment he looked as though he thought I was going to ask him for his temple recommend. I pulled a chair right close to him and looked into his eyes and said, "Young man, I want to ask you a very serious question."

"Oh, yes, sir," he said. "Go right ahead."

"Now, without pulling any punches, what do you and your parents think about the Athanasian Creed?"

He looked at me and got as worried as I have ever seen a young fellow, and he said, "Oh, I don't know, Brother Dunn, but I didn't do it. It must be some of those other kids I'm running around with."

Well, I trust you're learning your lessons better than most! We have a chance to see you at close range, and I like what I see. The youth of the Church are offering tremendous assets to the world.

President McKay

I had an opportunity to visit with President David O. McKay one morning. I told him briefly that I would have a chance to speak at a BYU devotional that morning, and the thought of speaking to youth always brightened his day.

A few weeks earlier I had the opportunity to take three young people to see him in his hotel apartment. He and Sister McKay were occupying twin wheelchairs as we entered the living room. He chatted with each of these young people about their aspirations and goals and how they were preparing for life. It was a tender scene, to be sure. Then as he took his seat again in the wheelchair (for he had insisted upon standing), we quietly excused ourselves.

A member of his family had come in to announce that the car was ready in the garage to take them to Huntsville. This man, who understood the gospel and its purposes, had a tremendous zest for life. He leaned over and patted his wife on the hand and said, "Come on, honey, I'll race you to the parking lot."

I would only hope that we could keep as interested in life and the future as he was.

Youth and a Bright Future

I want to share with you a feeling that has been burning within me for some time now. As I travel around the world, I see the Church and the gospel at work in different countries. I appreciate with you that we have some international concerns in the world. I know full well that these are the last days. But I am also encouraged by what I see in the world.

From my vantage point where the horizon can be seen, I see our youth's future is bright. I personally believe that our youth will live long enough to get married and bring children into the world. I think our youth will live long enough to be grandparents. These are my feelings. We're talking in the Church about programs and plans that project themselves well into the future.

Sometimes I get a little concerned about the "gloom prophets" in our midst. I know that we have to sound the warning and I appreciate that we must call the world to repentance, but I can also assure our youth that their future is reasonably bright and hopeful. I would like our youth to know that I feel very good about where they are going and how they are going to fit in. I like what I see.

I appreciate too that in the Far East the picture has not always been bright. Nor did it a few years ago when some of us viewed World War II and some of the other international conflicts. Sure, we have problems. We came to this earth to solve our problems; that is our purpose here. May I encourage you to plan for your future. It will come! Look at the positive side of life.

Lincoln Versus Lenin

I hope we think often about the value of our country and about the patriotic teachings of the gospel. Recently I came across an article in the *Week* magazine written by a man named Robert Kazmayer. He had just come from visiting Russia, where, as I suppose many spectators do, he had viewed the tomb of Lenin. He made some observations that I think are pertinent to one's point of view and serve to remind us of our great American heritage. These are his words:

> *I thought of the contrast between [Lincoln and Lenin]. You go down into the darkness in Lenin's Tomb. At the Lincoln Memorial you ascend the steps in the light. You look down at Lenin; you raise your eyes to Lincoln. I don't want to be melodramatic about this thing, but there is a contrast between those two leaders, Lenin and Lincoln. Lenin spent his whole life setting class against class. Abraham Lincoln said, "You can't help the poor by attempting to destroy the rich. You can't raise up the wage earner by pulling down the wage payer."*
>
> *Lenin said, "One would like to caress the masses, but one doesn't dare: like a dog they will turn and bite." Abraham Lincoln said, "God must have loved the common people: he made so many of them."*
>
> *Lenin said, "This is a fight to the end, to their extinction—and yours and mine and all who will not bow to the hammer and sickle." Abraham Lincoln said, "With malice toward none; with charity for all."*
>
> *Lenin said, "There's nothing right or wrong in the world, there's nothing false or true, except as it furthers the revolution." That's dialectical materialism for you. Abraham Lincoln said, "With firmness in the right as God gives us to see the right."*

I have appreciated those words as I have reflected upon the life of one great American. I have sensed a

deeper appreciation, having walked on a few of those bat-
tlefields myself and knowing firsthand the great price that
young men are paying today in order that we might be
free people.

An Interest in the Future

Now may I change the scene for a moment. I mentioned earlier how positive I feel the future will be in your
lives. Someone has said, "I am intensely interested in the
future because I expect to spend the rest of my days there."
I hope you have that same interest. The past is something
we can forget. We can learn from it certainly, but the future is the period of our lives we need to ponder.

Frequently I have a number of young people call on
me, and I appreciate their confidence and thoughtfulness
and their faith that together we might share feelings. Many
have told me there are times in their lives when they get
down in the dumps, a little bit discouraged, wondering
whether life is really worthwhile. Some even wonder
whether or not the sacrifice they are now making to gain
an education is worth the effort.

Four Basic Ingredients

I have thought along these lines a little bit of late, and
I would like to share with you four basic ingredients that
I have found extremely vital in living a happy, secure, and
peaceful life.

Whether you are going to be an athlete, a business
executive, an advertising man, or a successful housewife,
or whether you are talking about marriage relationships
or the professions, I have found that these four things
bring success and happiness to all who follow where they
lead. They are not threats; they are basic laws of life.

Dedication

The first ingredient I would mention is dedication, commitment to a cause, the giving of oneself wholeheartedly to the effort.

I remember some years ago I sat in the presence of President McKay when he was calling me to my present position. We visited for a few moments to put me at ease, and then the prophet went on to test for dedication. This is the way he put it, "Now, Brother Dunn, I am calling you to a position for the rest of your life. Before you answer yes or no, you tell me whether you are willing to put everything you have on the altar of God. Everything!" ("Are you that committed?" he wanted to know.)

I thought, "The rest of my life!" It seemed like my life was going to terminate momentarily, but if I lived the full span, he was asking if I would be willing to give everything for the next thirty or forty years. I thought about it; my whole life passed through my mind. I remember (this shows you how human my mind can be at times) I had, I think, seven dollars in my wallet. I thought, "Well, that won't be much of a sacrifice; he can certainly have that." I remember thinking about what little talent might exist in this puny life of mine; he could certainly have all of that.

But then I contemplated time and energy. That was something entirely different!

President McKay was simply saying, "Now, Brother Dunn, I want you to dedicate yourself to the Lord. Will you? Are you that committed?"

You know the answer. Dedicating one's life to a good cause is a prerequisite to success.

Dedication to a Cause—Lou Brisse

Young people are in the preparatory stages of life. Whether planning marriage or a profession, they need the ingredient of dedication. Unless you are committed to your cause, your reaping the happiness and success harvest will be nil. To be sure, dedication is a basic ingredient of a successful life.

I don't know how many of you remember Lou Brisse, former southpaw pitcher for the Philadelphia Athletics some years ago. Here was a young man who had dedication. I happen to have gone into professional baseball the same year Lou did. We were of comparable age, graduating from high school at the same time. Lou was a competitor's competitor. He was a hungry ballplayer, as we used to say. He wanted to go to the top, and he was committed to doing it.

Well, as many may know, 1942 was a bleak period. That was when World War II really started to spread and eighteen-year-olds were being drafted. Lou was one of these. He went over to Sicily with the infantry. On one of the beachheads he got hit in the right leg with a fragment from a German 88mm shell. The blast nearly took his leg off. As Lou lay on the beach literally bleeding to death in a semiconscious state, he heard one of the field doctors say, "We'll have to take his leg off."

He gained just enough strength to say, "No! Please leave it on. I've got to earn a living as a ballplayer. Leave it, even though it is useless."

The doctor answered, "We will do what we can."

Back to the field hospital he went. After many operations they put a steel plate in his leg and sent him home for many more operations. You would think that would discourage most people in this world, wouldn't you?

Well, in 1946 Lou was finally released from his medical labors. He limped with a cane and reported back to Connie Mack and the Philadelphia ball club. "Connie, can I have my job back? The government says that's the arrangement."

Connie looked at his leg and with little hope said, "Sure, you can come and play with us."

So that year Lou worked out with the Athletics. In the spring of 1947 I happened to be in the training camp just a couple of fields away from where Lou was playing. They let him suit up that year. He went out with a bit of a limp, and through a rugged training program, he got himself into shape.

To make my point, on opening day at Fenway Park in Boston Connie Mack walked out with that brand new baseball and handed it to Lou and said, "Lou, you have earned the right to start the game today." Lou walked out on the mound. Can you imagine the thrill that came to Lou standing on the mound after such a struggle?

Lou got the first two batters out without any trouble. The third hitter that day was Ted Williams. Ted Williams was no slouch. I know; I have pitched to him a time or two, and if you ever want a lesson in humility, he can give it! As he leveled off that bat, Ted hit the third pitch—a screaming line drive right back to the pitcher's box. It caught Lou on the right leg where the steel plate was embedded and threw him to the ground. He lay writhing on the mound in agony. I suppose none can contemplate the pain.

At that point, most people would quit, saying, "Why do I get all the problems?" "I'm discouraged. I'll throw in the towel." Not Lou Brisse. No, he was committed to a cause. He had a purpose in life. And he crawled to his knees as old Connie Mack walked out to him and said, "Give me the ball, Lou. We'd better not take any more chances."

Lou objected. "Don't take me out. You know how long I have had to fight to come back."

"Sure, we know," Connie replied. "Think you can get to your feet?"

"Yes, sir."

With pain I suppose we can't measure, Lou stood and threw the next pitch. He finished that inning and the next. Finally in the bottom half of the ninth inning, the score was Philadelphia 4, Boston 2. It is one of the great comeback stories of all time. Lou registered sixteen wins that year because he would not quit. He had that commitment, that dedication to a cause.

That is what makes a success—not quitting. Stay down when you fall and you are a loser. Get up one more time and you will win. There is no disgrace in falling; it is lying there that defeats us. The life of every great person is full of discouragement—falling, failing. Getting up is what makes the winner. I love the life of Lou Brisse, who has taught me a great deal in the area of commitment.

Understanding Self

The second ingredient has to do with understanding—understanding of self first, knowing who you are, what you are, what you are about. I don't need to convince you who you are. We believe and teach to the world that we are literally the offspring of an eternal Heavenly Father and Mother. What more glorious message can the world have than that? Do you think you are destined to failure—you, an offspring of an Eternal Parent? Nay, verily. The assurance that God is our literal Father is a basic ingredient for success in this life.

The Lord cares about you and about me and will do all He can through revelation and prayer to bring us up to be like Him. Do you think you have the capacity to become perfect? That is what we teach, isn't it? The Lord said, "Be ye therefore perfect." (Matthew 5:48.) This verse does not say that we are perfect, but it suggests that we have the capacity within us to become perfect. Do you think that you should be a college dropout, that you have to settle for a D in some class? No, you have the power, the capacity, to succeed. It is a matter of application once you understand who you are and the purpose for which you have come.

Confidence in self is one of the great ingredients of a successful life. If I were to ask you what you fear most in life, it wouldn't be getting out on the ball field or driving on the freeway or even going to war. Sure, the thoughts of these may give you butterflies, but what you fear most in this life is yourself. "What do people think of me? How do I react? What is my image? Am I acceptable to the group? Will he like me? How does she feel about me?" These are the concerns that we all have. Through the gospel of Jesus Christ we can come to understand ourselves for what we are and thus resolve such concerns.

There is not a person in the world who is more fearful of a group than I am, but I am confident in the knowledge that I am literally an offspring of an eternal Father and Mother. This assurance gives me courage to do things that I would not do on my own. An understanding of the great gospel principles alters our lives and makes us what we can become.

Understanding the Gospel

We need also to understand the gospel and its vital role in our lives. Several years ago a few institute directors heard President McKay make an interesting statement. "Brethren," he said, "I am concerned about the future of the Church as it relates to understanding the gospel and the lives of our people. One of the greatest single challenges facing the Latter-day Saint people is spiritual illiteracy. Our people know a lot about facts and history, but many have not yet caught the true meaning of the principles and how to apply them to life." Then he challenged us to see what we could do to help correct this.

Understanding Others

I think we also need to understand others, our fellowmen, and to lose ourselves in the service of others. That is one of the messages of the Savior (a message that is frequently overlooked)—to lose oneself, once he finds out who he is, in the service of others.

A Dedicated Home Teacher

I would like to share a little experience that happened some time ago in our home. I had a home teacher whom I wish we could put on a mimeograph and run off for the whole Church. I hope your home teacher has an understanding of people and a commitment to the cause like mine did. He was not a professional educator; he was a self-made businessman, but he was dedicated and he understood himself and others.

He was assigned to visit our family. (I can appreciate that he might have had some concern getting the name of a General Authority. You know, "All the names in the Church and I draw one of these brethren!") He called me on the telephone. "Brother Dunn," he said, "I have been assigned to be your new home teacher. I am wondering if we could set up a schedule that would be conducive to you and to me." So we agreed that the following Thursday would be his first visit. We set it for 7:30, giving us time to clear up the dinner dishes and get the family together. At 7:20 on the appointed night, I got the front room ready and turned on the porch light.

Then I walked over to the dining room window, where the curtains were drawn, and waited for my home teacher to come. About twenty-five minutes after the hour, a car pulled up, the headlights went out, and I could see that he and his fifteen-year-old companion were having a word of prayer. So I too bowed my head at the window and prayed that the Dunns might be receptive and that our visitors might have the courage of their convictions to present their message and challenge.

I watched them get out of the car, and then I quickly backed away from the window and waited for the bell to ring. When I heard the doorbell, I waited about thirty seconds before stepping to the door and opening it.

"Good evening, Brother Dunn," he said and then introduced me to his young companion. I escorted them into the front room and went and got my wife and one daughter. Then I made a parental faux pas—I called to the daughter who was downstairs. "Can you come up, honey?" I called gently. "Home teachers are here."

Then came that resounding voice from the basement, "How long is it going to be?"

So I went down and brought her upstairs. She asked again on the way, "My favorite program is on. How long are they going to be?"

"We owe it to them," I said. "Let's go in, honey."

The family gathered around, and our home teacher began. I could tell he was nervous, but because he cared about people, he had taken time to learn a little bit about each one of my family members. He started out with little Kellie. She was about five then. He said, "Kellie, I understand that Miss Finlinson is your kindergarten teacher. Is that right?"

"That's right."

"What is your favorite subject?"

This little girl started to open up and talk. It usually took days to get her going the way she did then. But he was right there with her. He asked about Candy and Pam, her girl friends—because he cared and had taken the time to find out about Kellie's particular interests. He could lose himself in others.

He went on to visit with my second daughter. He knew a little about her life and some of her other interests; he had found a level on which they could communicate.

I remember that he then turned to our oldest daughter and asked, "Is your dad holding family home evenings?"

There I was really on the spot. Under my breath I said, "Come on, honey, answer it right!"

"Yes," she said.

"Is it the kind of an experience that you like?"

"Sometimes."

He looked at me as though to ask, "Brother Dunn, what are you going to do to make it a good experience *all* the time?"

Addressing daughter number two, he asked, "Tell me, if your dad could make your family home evenings even better than they are, what would you suggest that he do?"

And do you know what that girl answered? She didn't even pause! "Could you get him to quit talking so much?"

He turned to me and said, "Did you get the message, Elder?"

I got it. You see, here was a man who understood what he was supposed to do. He understood the program. As they stood and were ready to leave, he asked, "May we kneel in prayer, Brother Dunn?"

A Family Spiritual Experience

So we knelt down and prayed. He left a beautiful spirit in our home. On the way to the door, he asked me,

"Brother Dunn, what specifically are you doing to give your family a spiritual experience every week?"

You know, that made me think. "Well, I come home once in a while," I answered.

"No," he said, "I mean different from that."

I said, "Well, other than what we try in our little family get-togethers, not too much. We pray together, we have fun together. I teach them many principles, but I don't know about a planned experience every time."

Then he challenged me to read the scriptures to my family and interpret them and have a good experience in this way. And that home teacher followed through and kept me committed until we increased the spirituality in our home—all this accomplished by a wonderful home teacher who understood people.

One week later this good brother called at our door unannounced.

I answered and was surprised to see him. "What are you doing here tonight?" I asked. "Have I forgotten the night of our appointment?"

"No," he said, "Could I see your daughter Marsha for just a minute?"

"Why, certainly," I said.

I escorted him into the front room and went out into the kitchen where Marsha was setting the table for dinner. "Marsha, our home teacher wants to see you."

"What did I do?"

"I don't know. Why don't you go see?"

So she tiptoed in. He wasn't a minute with her. I heard the front door shut as she came into the kitchen carrying a little box nicely gift wrapped. It was her birthday, and somebody besides the family cared enough to remember!

Pleased about his thoughtfulness, Marsha exclaimed, "Look!"

"What is it?" I asked.

"I don't know."

"Why not open it and find out?"

So she set it down and opened it, and there was a beautiful little corsage. The attached card said, "Happy birthday, Marsha. I've been thinking about you all day. Love, your home teacher."

How do you think she responded the next time he called? You see, this is one of the great keys to success in this life—the ability to lose yourself in the lives of others.

Skill

Let me just mention two other ingredients for successful living. The third ingredient is skill. Elbert Hubbard has said, "Folks who never do any more than they get paid for never get paid for any more than they do." Think about that. Your return and reward are in direct proportion to the talent and ability that you offer to the world.

Fritz Kreisler made this observation, "Life means my opportunity to serve humanity!"

And George Bernard Shaw said, "A gentleman is one who puts more into life than he takes out of it." I hope that is your philosophy.

I think about the sisters with the same interest and concern as I do the brethren, because their full potential cannot be realized until they develop their talents and skills.

Enthusiasm

Finally I would mention that wonderful ingredient we call enthusiasm. You know, you radiate what you are in this life.

A long time ago when I was an eighteen-year-old

baseball rookie coming from Hollywood High School to the Pocatello Cardinals in the old Pioneer League, I learned that one's talent, ability, understanding, and dedication are not effective until he can radiate enthusiasm.

Have you ever been impressed by the way some people radiate? Contrast in your mind the lack of impression left by people who do not radiate. Have you ever gone, as I have, into a classroom where the whole atmosphere seemed to communicate, "We are here to learn, so let's wade through this class hour somehow." Contrast that attitude with the enthusiasm of one who lives, who experiences, who radiates, who sets you on fire.

"I'm Gonna Help You"

That is what Nick Cullup, my former baseball manager, did to me. While I did not want to follow some of his personal habits, he was an enthusiastic, effective manager.

When three of us reported as rookies on the same day, he looked us over and said, "You fellows are supposed to be ballplayers?"

"Yep!" I showed him all my news clippings.

He wasn't impressed. "You don't *look* like what you are supposed to be."

"Kid," he continued, "when I put you on a ball field, I want you to *look* like something. You don't even know how to dress; you don't know how to walk; you don't know how to project yourself. Why, the opposing batters will have a field day on you! You have to learn to look mean and confident as well as to be skillful."

Time won't permit me to relate all the antics Nick put me through, but he taught me how to dress one day in front of a mirror—how to tuck my shirt in so that I looked like what I was supposed to be, how to beak the old cap, how to stand out on the mound and look mean at the batter. It was all part of radiating enthusiasm.

He was an old catcher from way back with the Washington Senators. His hands were knotted like the knots on a tree. That first day he walked out and said to me, "Kid, what's your best pitch?"

"Well," I said, "I can throw a fast ball and a good curve."

Then, without a catcher's mitt, he said, "Throw it to me. Give it all you've got."

I threw it—POW—and he said, "Is that *all* the harder you can throw?" (Now that really builds confidence, doesn't it?)

"I wouldn't mind if you played ball in my living room," he added. "You wouldn't hurt anything."

Then he said, "I'm gonna help you." So he had a big overstuffed catcher's mitt made that looked like something Al Shalk, the baseball clown, would carry out on the ball field. Nick used to soak this mitt in linseed oil, and then he would bake it and get it just so it was crisp. Every time I'd even throw a ball—POW—that thing would pop.

"Now when we get out on the field," he explained, "We're going to make you *sound* like what you're supposed to be. You're going to *radiate*, and the opponent is going to be so nervous that he'll drop 15 percent of his batting average when he sees you on the mound."

He taught me how to walk onto the field, how to look, how to observe, how to make the ball sound like it was moving twice as fast as it was—WHAM! The opponent soon got the message. Enthusiasm is what Nick Cullup taught me, and that's the key to success. You radiate what you are!

A Special Witness

I know that God is real, that Jesus is the Christ, that this *is* the gospel that He brought to earth and has restored through prophets in these latter days. When you feel downhearted and discouraged, I want you to know that there are those who do not waver. We have been through some of these struggles before you. I want you to know that it is worth the price you are paying in time and energy.

CHAPTER 7

Know Thyself, Control Thyself, Give Thyself

During the time I was associated with the institute program in southern California, I often had opportunities to visit with dignitaries. On one occasion we were in the process of doing some remodeling in our institute building, and I was reviewing some bids from very important establishments.

I had an appointment one morning with a representative from one of the better-known firms, and right at the appointed hour a knock came at my door. I opened it, and standing in the framework was a very interesting-looking character. Even though he was in the building, he still had his hat on; his tie and shirt had parted company; and from the aroma that came from him, I could tell that he had just disposed of a cigar before coming in.

"Good morning," he said with all the firmness I have ever seen in a man. And taking me by the hand, he said, "My name is Joseph Smith."

I was startled. I wondered what he was up to and thought, "Two can play this game." So I just squared my shoulders and put out my chin and said, "I'm glad to meet you, Joseph. I am Brigham Young."

He really looked shocked, and then he gave me shock number two. He reached into his pocket and pulled out a business card. He represented the firm I was expecting, and his name really was Joseph Smith!

Then I didn't have the heart to tell him that I wasn't Brigham Young, and so all during the conversation he kept saying, "Yes, Mr. Young. Thank you, Mr. Young." I can imagine what he must have told his cronies back at the office.

The "Nephite" Visitor

I once had another rather interesting introduction. When I first moved to Downey, California, I hadn't been in my new stake more than a few days when the stake president called and, as they often do, enlisted me in a new assignment on the stake Sunday School board. Very quickly I was introduced to the stake superintendent, and he gave me two assignments for the following week. I was in a whole new area and didn't know anybody or any landmarks. But trying to be dutiful to my calling, I went to the ward I thought I was assigned to visit. I later found that two wards were located on the same street on opposite ends of town.

I walked in but found I was tardy by about fifteen minutes. As fate would have it, there wasn't a seat left in the congregation. So I thought I would take my place on the stand. A man was talking, and as I walked to the stand, I must have embarrassed him because he stopped and watched me go up. I hurried and took my seat and lowered my head so the pressure would pass.

Then the speaker said something a few minutes later that told me I was in the wrong ward.

"Oh, good heavens," I thought. "What should I do now? I need to make my report. I've got to go visit the other ward." Then it struck me that nobody knew me—I was a new board member in a new stake—so I quickly got up and walked out while the same fellow was still talking. I hurried on and found the right ward and completed my assignment.

The following Tuesday when I went to stake Sunday School board meeting to report, the superintendent was so excited that he grabbed me when I walked in. "Do you know what happened in our stake?" he asked.

"No, what happened?"

"Well, last Sunday we had a spiritual experience we'll always remember."

"Oh! What was that?"

He said, "Do you know that at such-and-such ward (the ward I had walked into first) they had a visit from one of the Three Nephites?"

Now let me introduce a six-word formula that, when applied to your life, will bring great joy and success.

Six Great Words

I would like to share with you six of the greatest words ever spoken, maybe by way of guidelines for the days, the weeks, and hopefully the years that lie ahead. These words are not original with me (few things are), but I would like to pass them along for the value they have had in my life and counsel you to follow their wisdom.

"Know Thyself"

One of the great teachers of all time, a philosopher in Greece, gave us the first two words of our formula. They are consistent with what this Church teaches today. Socrates said, "Know thyself." Know who you are and what you are, and plan accordingly.

Sometimes intellectually we have an understanding that we are the children of God, but our actions are not always consistent with this understanding. The knowledge of that principle has been very helpful to me, because I am the type of person who reaches a high peak once in a while, but then occasionally I get down in the valley of despair. I have been known to get discouraged. I even have a tendency on occasions to want to throw in the towel because things aren't going just exactly the way I think they should.

Still Struggling

At these times I am reminded of the great truth of rates. To know oneself is to know each of us is a child of God. We were not sent to mortality to fail; we were sent here to succeed. We have the capacity to win in whatever we attempt to tackle—whether it be on the ball field, in class, in life, in business, in marriage. A good Latter-day Saint who understands this basic tenet of the gospel cannot fail, because there is too much at stake when he comes to know who he really is.

Now just knowing such a principle doesn't mean it will lift you to great heights—it is a matter of discovery and application. I am still struggling. There are times when responsibilities become so heavy, and the human tendency is to quit, to check out, to remove the pressure. But the divine tendency is to stick, to fight, to renew, to repent, to stand, and to be courageous. That is why I am grateful to be affiliated with a Church that stands for sticking to a task until it is done.

All Can Achieve

There are always some who are discouraged and others who have great aspirations to achieve great heights.

May I assure you, from my own experience and as I have come to know the gospel of Jesus Christ, that everyone can achieve the very fullest in life. There is no such thing as a failure in life. We can all achieve when we understand our true role and potential.

I appreciate that environmental conditioning and exposure can set processes at work in all of us that keep us discouraged or downtrodden. But I assure you that you can do anything you want to do in this life. It isn't easy—it wasn't intended to be. In order to become like unto our Heavenly Father, we took upon ourselves a very heavy responsibility to come into mortality to work out our salvation. And hard work and experience and sweat became the formula.

The formula consists of keeping our Heavenly Father's commandments—living the gospel, listening to the counsel of our leaders, applying that counsel in our lives, and preparing ourselves mentally, physically, and spiritually. We have the capacity within us to become like Him, and you will if you will apply the formula and learn to "Know thyself."

"Control Thyself"

Some years later Cicero gave us the second two words of the formula. He said very simply and most profoundly, "Control thyself." It is one thing to know who you are, but it is another thing to control the capacity that you have.

Control, the Key in Baseball

A long time ago as a kid in the sand lots, I learned that blazing speed for a pitcher in baseball was not the key to pitching. Any good ballplayer will tell you that the key is control. You need speed for sure—you need a good curve ball and some other assets—but control is the first line of defense for a good pitcher.

Bob Feller

Bob Feller is a good example of this principle. Feller had a very unique ability as a young Iowa ballplayer. At sixteen years of age, Bob could throw a nine-inch baseball harder and faster than anyone else. I think he was clocked at about 105 miles an hour. (A nine-inch ball coming from a distance of 60 feet 6 inches at 105 miles an hour is about the size of an aspirin tablet—in fact, if you got in its way, you would need the tablet!) By way of comparison and to give you some idea, a pitcher like Sandy Koufax threw a baseball at approximately 95 miles an hour, or "Bullett" Bob Turley at about 90 miles an hour.

But Bob Feller had a problem as a sixteen-year-old boy. With that blazing speed, he couldn't control the ball. He would just throw it all over the park. When you are at the plate, it makes quite a difference where the ball is coming. Bob was great, not because he could throw harder than anybody else, but because he listened to counsel from some great teachers who were close to him.

His coaches said, "Bob, there's one lesson you've got to learn if you're going to stick. If you want to be a great ballplayer, you will need to take a little speed off your fastball and in the process learn how to control it. You've got to find the strike zone."

Bob Feller listened to counsel, and that is why he is where he is today.

Jim Rusick

Jim Rusick was a teammate of mine at Hollywood High. He was 225 pounds, 6 feet 3 inches, half-American, half-Indian, and he could also throw a nine-inch baseball 105 miles an hour. But Jim Rusick never made it in the big leagues. He had the same talent and the same speed, but Jim wouldn't listen to counsel. He didn't learn to control the ability he had.

How We Aim

We all have the capacity to achieve if we will aim in the right direction. That, to me, is the glorious thing about the gospel of Jesus Christ. Every soul has the capacity to go all the way—whether we do or not depends on how we use and aim our abilities. The Lord said: "Be ye therefore perfect." (Matthew 5:48.) He has instilled in each of us the desire and the capacity, and you and I can achieve it!

Sometimes it seems that we are deluged with arbitrary rules and programs, but they are for only one good reason. Therein is the strike zone in being an effective player in life. I have come to know in my exposure as a player on the Lord's team that if I follow His counsel, I will not go very wrong.

A Latter-day Saint Girl on a College "Holiday"

I often see young people aim at their targets, and sometimes they tend to miss the mark. This naturally brings concern to parents and leaders alike.

I knew a young girl at the University of Southern California who came from a wonderful Latter-day Saint home. Her father was in a very responsible position, but, like lots of young people who go away from home, she thought she would take the proverbial Roman holiday. So on her religious preference card she put "Protestant," instead of standing up to be counted and putting "Latter-day Saint." She thought she would get away for a little breather.

I learned from another Latter-day Saint student that she was on campus, so I went to visit her.

She was living in a big fancy sorority house that was lavishly furnished with a big winding, beautifully decorated staircase, and as I rang the bell, the chimes sounded all over the place.

I was ushered in and she was summoned. I'll never forget that experience. Little Jan descended the stairway holding a long cigarette holder in her hand, and attached to it was a king-size cigarette.

She was very proud and flippant about it, and as she came into my presence, she said in a very sophisticated voice, "Yeaaa-s?"

I said, "Jan, I'm Brother Paul Dunn, your institute director."

"Oh," she said, "I've had enough church!" And she took a big puff and blew the smoke back in my face.

It was all I could do to hold my patience. But I mustered up courage and looked at her and said, "Just so you will know, Jan, we have a wonderful program here. I have been commissioned by the Lord through His prophets to be your caretaker. I want you to know that we need you, and I think you need us."

"No," she said. "Thank you anyway. I've had enough church. In fact, I'd appreciate it if you wouldn't bother me. Take my name off your records."

Well, I couldn't do that because I knew of her capacity to become a true daughter of the Lord. So I commenced to work out a plan for her in my mind.

Fortunately she was in a four-year program, and every week for the next four years she either saw me or got a telephone call or a letter. I used to pull her card—I had access to it from the dean's file because I was the campus chaplain for the Latter-day Saints—and I would find out in what building and at what time she was in a particular class. Then I would just "happen" to be there when class let out.

When we'd bump into each other, I'd say, "Jan! How are you?"

"Oh, you again?"

"Why don't you come on over? We're having a great time."

"No. Thank you anyway, Brother Dunn, but I just can't work you in. I can't find the time—I'm just too busy."

Well, to make a long story short, in the last semester of the fourth year a knock came at my door at the institute. I opened it, and in the framework stood Jan. For a moment I was speechless. Then I said, "I'm honored, Jan, that you would come."

"I thought you might be," she said. "Where do you sign up?"

I said, "Are you serious?"

"Yes, sir."

I said, "May I ask just what motivated you to take a class?"

She said, "Very simple. I thought it was easier to sign up for a class and get you off my back."

I was flattered. She took the class.

A year and a half later an interesting event transpired. I had been called to Salt Lake, and Jan had met a wonderful dental student in our program. One day a call came on the phone, and Jan said, "Brother Dunn, would you honor us with your presence in the temple?"

I replied, "I'd be honored, Jan."

And that wonderful day arrived. Kneeling before the holy altar in one of our sealing rooms in the Salt Lake Temple was this girl, holding hands with a great young man who had all that any girl would desire. And by the authority of the holy Melchizedek Priesthood, I had the sacred privilege of uniting that pair for time and all eternity.

As I felt the Holy Spirit, I couldn't help but reflect back on that day so many years before when she had descended the stairway and, in that rather sophisticated sort of fashion, and, "yeaaa-s, what may I do for you?" The very scene before me was what I had desired for her —and that is the target I desire for everyone, and no one has to compromise.

"Give Thyself"

Let me give you the last two words of the formula. Jesus himself said, "Give thyself." We must remember who we are; we must aim our potential in that direction. But then we must give it to the Lord for the right reasons.

The Right Things for the Right Reasons

Some years ago President Harold B. Lee gave a very profound talk. He said, "Do the right thing for the right reason." I like that. You are preparing yourselves for great lives. And whether you are going to be a doctor, lawyer, teacher, engineer, or housewife, dedicate yourself to the Lord and you will be a happy, contented, wonderful Latter-day Saint.

The Football "Hero"

A great athlete who was a member of the Church took a class from me at the University of Southern California some years ago. He was a big fellow about 6 feet 4 inches and 220 pounds—an all-American boy from the physical standpoint. He was at USC on a fully paid four-year football scholarship. And he had a right, for he had earned it. Everybody clamored for him. I think he could have gone to any one of twenty colleges.

This boy had one problem—he thought he was the only thing that existed. And as he walked around the campus, he gave that air of authority. The only reason he came to the institute was that I had a class at noon that contained twenty-plus girls and two fellows. That was his motivation!

He used to time his entrance into class just following the opening prayer, and he would plop down on the back row and put his feet up on an adjoining chair. Then a sneer would come on his face that suggested, "Brother Dunn, I'm here. I dare you to teach me."

Did you ever see a student like that? It is a real challenge to a teacher, I promise you. Try as I would—I put on floor show after floor show for him—I couldn't penetrate his shell. He was just too hard, because he was turned in, selfish. The only time he would look interested was if we were honoring him at some event or a banquet.

Talk about discouragement! I would go home and tell my wife, "I'm through. I quit! I can't teach!" That would usually be about Thursday or Friday.

And she would grab me by the arm and say, "You can! Go get him!"

By Monday morning I would charge back saying, "I'm going to get that boy!"

By Wednesday, down in the valley of despair I'd go, "I can't! I can't!" I guess I resigned every week for six weeks.

The Orthopedic Ward

Then one day I got a telephone call from a very close friend of mine in Hollywood. He had a little baby that was born prematurely and wasn't expected to live. They had it in an incubator at the Hollywood Children's Hospital, and he wondered if I would hurry over and help administer to

it and give it a name and a blessing before it passed on. I
was honored and hurried over to the hospital.

In my anxiety to get to the floor where the incubators
were located, I got off one floor too soon. And, lo and behold, I found myself standing in the orthopedic ward of
the Hollywood Children's Hospital—thirty little beds
lined up. I was deeply touched when I saw all those little
children confined, many of them with crippled bodies.

So after completing the administration, I came back
to take a second look at those little children, and again
it affected me very deeply. This time I noticed they had
some volunteers working with them. I stepped up to the
desk and asked the nurse, "What's going on here?"

She said, "Well, we have a program where two days a
week people from the community come in and try to
brighten the children's day."

"How do you get involved?"

She said, "It is easy. Sign right here."

Now I took the pen to put down my own name, but I
couldn't. I felt impressed to put my athletic student's
name. So I wrote his name in place of mine.

She said thank you and called me by his name.

I had signed for the following Thursday at six o'clock
in the evening, but I didn't have the heart to go tell him
what I had done. He was the type of person who would
have refused if you asked him, because we weren't honoring him. So I waited until five o'clock on the following
Thursday, which was the date of our appointment. Then
I called him on the phone, and his mother answered.

I said, "Is Bill there?"

She said, "Yes, we're just ready to sit down to supper."

I said, "May I speak with him for a minute?"

"Certainly."

Bill came to the phone and said, "Hello?"

So I just reared back and said, *"Bill!* Will you help me, please?"

He said, "Oh, yes, sir. Yes, sir. But who is it?"

I said, "It's your institute teacher, Brother Dunn. Thank you. I'll be by and pick you up in fifteen minutes." And I hung up.

Well, I wish you could have been in the car with me. I drove over, and he was standing out on the curb. He had his letterman's sweater on, all three stripes showing, and a fourth of an apple pie in his hand.

I pulled over to the curb, opened the door, and said, "Get in quick."

He said, "What's the matter?"

I said, "Get in and I'll tell you."

He got in and slammed the door, and I think he thought we had just received a call to go back to Missouri. Then I sped off, knowing that when I did tell him, he would probably bail out.

I got around the corner doing about forty, and he said, "What's the excitement?"

I said, "Bill, I really appreciate you."

He said, "For what? For what?"

I said, "You're going down to the children's hospital and read to some kids."

He said, "I'm what?" Well, he wouldn't talk to me the rest of the trip.

When we got to the hospital, I literally pushed him out on the sidewalk. I gave him a note—third floor and the name of the nurse—and drove off and left him.

I said, "I'll be back in an hour to get you. The Lord bless you."

Well, an hour later I came back, and out of that hospital door walked a new man. When he got in the car, he couldn't talk.

I said, "Well, how did it go, Bill?"

"I can't tell you."

I said, "I understand. Don't try, but when you get your composure, let me know." So I turned on the car radio so the silence wouldn't be so obvious and we drove around for about ten minutes.

Then he turned off the radio and said, "Brother Dunn, that is one of the greatest experiences of my life."

I said, "I thought it would be. What happened?"

He said, "They assigned me to a little three-year-old girl who was born with part of a spine. She has never known a day out of bed. And that little girl was happier than I am. What's the matter with me?" (I wanted to tell him, but that wasn't the place.) Then he went on to say that he was given a chair by the side of the bed, and all the time he was reading she wanted to hold his hand. He read to her out of a giant pop-up Pinnochio book.

He said, "You know, it is embarrassing to read to kids, particularly when people can hear you. But, you know, after I finished the first page, I didn't care who heard me." Then he went on to say he finished that story and another and another, until finally it was time to go.

He said, "Brother Dunn, I got ready to go, and the little girl didn't want me to. She pulled me down, and you know her whole hand barely fit around one of my fingers. Then she gave me a kiss on the nose and asked me to come back next week. Brother Dunn, you might think I'm a nut, but I signed up for another month."

"No, I don't think you're a nut, Bill. This is what we've been trying to talk about in class. See, you can talk about theories and lesson plans all you want, but you found out what the Lord said, as Luke recorded it—when you lose yourself in the service of others, you find the real you. This is the greatness of the gospel."

A Discovery

Bill discovered it in his nineteenth year. Two weeks later a knock came at my door, and he filled the whole framework. I said, "What is it, Bill? What can I do to help you?"

"Well," he said, "I've really done it this time."

"What did you do?"

He said, "I just resigned my scholarship—four years!"

"Now why did you do that?"

"I just accepted a mission call. I'm going out and kind of lose myself."

I spoke at his farewell, and two years later when he returned, he blessed me with a little visit. When Bill came back, he was still 6 feet 4 inches tall and 220 pounds, but he had a spirit to match it. What a great contribution he will make to the world, to the Church, because he followed the admonition of the Savior.

Six Great Words

Find out who you are: "Know thyself." Control the energy and capacity that the Lord has blessed you with: "Control thyself." Then give it to the world: "Give thyself." That is the success formula I would counsel you to follow. It is true!

CHAPTER 8

The Quality of Happiness

Kellie and Happiness

I had the opportunity, along with my wife, to go to my daughter's elementary school to review the work of the previous semester. (That is always interesting to a parent, because he is anxious to see his child's work as compared with that of her peer group.)

On this particular night they were displaying some of the recent artwork the children had completed. The theme they had selected to illustrate was one that is quite popular. The assignment was for each child to define the meaning of happiness. I remember looking at one poster and seeing that happiness was being invited to the circus. The child had drawn a picture of clowns and balloons and a large interesting tent. Happiness on the next poster had something to do with going to a ball game.

Then I very excitedly looked for Kellie's poster, and found it at last. On it she had drawn a picture of a very interesting-looking figure for a father and had written, "Happiness is when Dad comes home at night." Can you appreciate a little what that did to me as a father?

During an illness this same little daughter asked me

to pick up a record she had been wanting for sometime. It was a catchy tune all about happiness. We heard the record something like three or four thousand times in the next few days. She loved the tune—it was a lively one and had a pretty good beat. "Happiness is," it suggested, "different things to different people." This is what the record said:

> *To the preacher, it's a prayer, prayer, prayer.*
> *To the Beatles, it's a yeah, yeah, yeah.*
> *To a golfer, it's a hole-in-one.*
> *To a father, it's a brand new son.*
> *To a sailor, it's the sea, sea, sea.*
>
> *To my mother, why it's me, me, me.*
> *To the birdies, it's the sky above.*
> *But in my life, it's the one I love.*
> *Happiness is different things to different people.*

Signs and Happiness

One day while driving I noticed a very interesting signboard that said, "Happiness is owning an electric dryer." I drove a little farther and there was another happiness sign that said that you weren't completely happy until you owned a certain model of car. I didn't know that, and since my model wasn't one of theirs, I was supposed to be miserable.

"Dear Abby" and Happiness

I guess all these things about happiness have caused me to be a bit on the alert. So I was naturally interested when "Dear Abby" wrote about happiness. Abby had just received a letter from a young lady who defined her ideas concerning happiness. Let me share it with you. The girl said:

Happiness is knowing your parents won't almost kill you if you come home a little late at night.
Happiness is having your own bedroom.
Happiness is having parents that trust you.
Happiness is getting the phone call that you have been praying for all day.
Happiness is getting good grades, and making your parents proud of you.
Happiness is being included in the most popular circle.
Happiness is in having parents who don't fight.
Happiness is knowing that you are as well dressed as anyone else.
Happiness is something I don't have.
(Signed) Fifteen and Unhappy

Abby was quite smart in her response. Rather than answering the letter directly, she invited the reading audience to submit their responses. Let me share a few of their replies.

Here is one:

Dear Fifteen and Unhappy: Happiness is coming home on time so your parents won't worry. Happiness is having someone to share a bedroom with. Happiness is proving to your parents that you can be trusted. Happiness is in realizing that sometimes you are lucky that you don't get what you pray for. Happiness is including someone who is lonely and unpopular in your circle. Happiness is having parents who stay together in spite of disagreements. Happiness is keeping the clothes you have neat and clean and not worrying about how they measure up to somebody else. Happiness is not something you get, it is something you give.
(Signed) Fifteen and Happy

Here is another from Vietnam:

Dear Abby: We're a bunch of guys in Vietnam doing a job for Uncle Sam and we read your column in Stars and Stripes *the other day. That fifteen-year-old kid sure has a lot to learn, doesn't she? Do you know what happiness is for kids out here? Happiness is having enough to eat so that when you go to sleep at night your stomach doesn't ache. Happiness is having shoes on your feet and any kind of clothing to keep the cold out. Happiness is having a roof over your head. Happiness is being able to get any kind of an education some time in your life. Happiness is believing that the dream of freedom, brotherhood, and peace for mankind will someday come.*

(Signed) Some Very Happy GI's

And then finally:

Dear Abby: Happiness is being able to walk. Happiness is being able to talk. Happiness is being able to see. Happiness is being able to hear. Unhappiness is reading a letter from a fifteen-year-old girl who can do all of these things and still isn't happy. I can talk and I can see and I can hear, but I can't walk, but I am thirteen and real happy.

(Signed) Thirteen and Happy

Happiness Is Different Things

Well, happiness is different things to different people. I think perhaps one of the great delusions in this whole area of what makes people happy ought to be looked at for a moment. May I just suggest that we take a real look within our own souls and see what happiness is to us.

Sometimes we think we will be happy:

When we arrive at a certain destination.

When our schooling is finished. (I remember completing the final touches on a doctoral degree some years ago.

I turned in the dissertation—a long anticipated moment—and I thought, "Oh, happiness will be in getting that degree and not worrying anymore about school. Look at all the time that will be mine!" What a laugh! I found that I got busier and busier and that true happiness wasn't in the completion, but in the commencing of a new way of life.)

When we get a better job.
When we arrive at a certain income.
When we are married.
When the baby is born.
When we recover from our illness.
When our bills are all paid.
When we own a new car.
When some disagreeable task is finished.
When we are free from all responsibilities.

A wise person has written, "Happiness is a journey, not a destination. Happiness is to be found along the way, not at the end of the road, for then the journey is over and it is too late. The time for happiness is today, not tomorrow."

Joseph Smith and Happiness

It was Joseph Smith who gave us a true understanding of what happiness really is. "Happiness," he said, "is the object and design of our existence; and will be the end thereof, if we pursue the path that leads to it; and this path is virtue, uprightness, faithfulness, holiness, and keeping all the commandments of God. . . . But we cannot keep all the commandments without first knowing them."

The Gospel and Happiness

May I add my opinion as to what I feel happiness is —some of the things I might pass along to you if I were creating a little poster along with Kellie to put on my bulletin board.

Happiness is knowing and completely understanding the gospel of Jesus Christ, as the Prophet Joseph Smith indicated, to the extent that we can make daily application of gospel principles in solving the problems of life. The Prophet was right in suggesting that coming to understand the commandments and keeping them bring real happiness. I know this to be true. Let me illustrate with a personal experience.

A Daughter and Gospel Principles

Sometime ago I had a challenge as a father when one of my daughters, during her junior high school days, came to me with a social problem that was very disturbing. At the time my daughter was involved with a social group of seven girls—four members of the Church and three nonmembers. The four had a silent pact, as it were, to try to convert the other three. As they were lunching together, as they frequently did, one of the young Latter-day Saint girls commenced to tell an off-colored story. It was in poor taste and totally out of order.

My daughter came home that night and recounted the situation—in fact, she was even bold enough to tell me the story. It was a problem! "Now," she said, "Dad, don't tell me what's right and what's wrong. I think I understand the principles of the gospel sufficiently to know that wasn't the thing to do. But what do you do when you find yourself in this kind of situation? How do you handle it?"

She didn't add this postscript, but I could see it in her eyes: "Remember, Dad, the important thing at my age is to be included. And remember too that every fifteen-year-old wants to be popular, to be accepted, to be wanted, and they don't want things to be too 'churchy.' " She was saying, in effect, "Will you give me an answer and at the same time keep me popular." (That is a real task for any teacher or parent!)

So we visited for a while. I turned, after some discussion, to the cleansing of the temple experience recorded in Matthew, Mark, and Luke. You will recall the story of the Pharisees, the Sadducees, and the practices of the money changers. (I didn't take a lot of time to give her the history or background, although there are times when the history is needed and helpful. Somehow she could still live in this life without all of the excess baggage, as it were. Oh, I am not trying to suggest that these things aren't important to know historically, but more important than knowing the dimensions of the Nauvoo Temple, more important than knowing how many missions we have in the Church, more important than knowing what exactly will occur in the millennial reign is the ability to apply divine principles daily so that life can be happy and truly enjoyed.) So as I read the cleansing of the temple story, I asked her, "What do you get out of this story?"

She said, "Well, the Savior was upset."

I said, "May I just suggest one thought. He was saying to his peer group that there comes a time in every person's life when he has to stand up and be counted, and while it may not be the popular thing to do, there are times when you have to do what's right even though it isn't easy. You may have to stand alone a few times. You think about that and then we'll have another talk."

She thought about it and came back a little while later and said, "I can't think of any way to apply the principle, Dad."

So we talked some more.

I said, "I'll tell you what—if the Savior were right, let's you and I go out to the garage and I'll make a cat-o-nine-tails whip so you can take it with you tomorrow and clean out that junior high school of all its iniquities."

"Dad," she said, "you have missed the point. You *can't* do that and be popular."

I said, "All right, how's this for an idea. How would it be the next time you find yourself in that kind of social situation and somebody starts to tell an off-colored story, if you stand up and say, 'Now you listen here, we won't have any more of that!' "

She said, "Dad, you just haven't got it! I couldn't do that!"

I thought maybe she would think that way, and so I said, "Well, now why don't *you* submit a plan?"

She said, "Let me think some more." She walked away with that look that said, "How did I ever get *you* for a dad!"

I went about my business. A new day came and went, and as I returned home the next day, I found my wife in the kitchen peeling potatoes for supper. As I approached her to give her a little kiss, I noticed she was holding back the tears. And I thought, "Potatoes don't do this."

"What's the matter, honey?"

She said, "It's your daughter. Better go see her."

I thought, "Another crisis!" So I tiptoed into the back bedroom, and there was a sweet experience awaiting me. This little lady, who had wrestled with life as it really is, was sitting on her bed pushing back a few tears of her own.

I said, "Well, tell me what the matter is."

She said, "Dad, it is an interesting thing. I took the cleansing of the temple story to task today and tried it out."

I said, "Oh, did you clean out the junior high?"

"No," she said, "I called the girl who had told the off-colored story and asked her to walk home with me. So we walked home, and I brought her into the bedroom and sat her down and said, 'I just want you to know that our friendship means a great deal to me. Yesterday you really put all of us on the spot. I felt it and I think you did. I know you didn't mean to cause feelings or tension, but when you told that story, it reduced all of us in the eyes of our non-Latter-day Saint friends. Now while I appreciate your intent was maybe honorable and you thought this was a clever way to be noticed, I wonder if next time you feel you have to do this you would warn me in advance so I can be excused?"

Then she told me how her friend broke down and put her arms around her and said, "Will you forgive me?"

It Really Works!

She said, "Dad, we cried for a while." Then the climax: "You know what, Dad?"

I said, "No, what?"

Then she said, "The New Testament really works, doesn't it?"

"Yes, the New Testament really works." When you come to understand the concepts and the principles contained in it and you make the proper application in life, it doesn't matter whether you are sitting in a parked car, whether you are at the ball game, whether you are in an athletic contest—you will be able to draw upon gospel principles and solve life's daily challenges and thus find the eternal joy and happiness that we each seek.

May I suggest that happiness, as I have come to know it and to appreciate it, is being able to discipline oneself to accept the standards of the gospel of Jesus Christ and make proper application of them to daily living.

Awards Unearned

I was sitting in my study at home reminiscing with

some old books and school records. As I was cleaning out a file that contained some old documents, lo and behold, I came upon two awards given me some twenty-plus years ago. They had gold seals attached, and you would normally think that a young man would be proud to have these in his possession. That would be true if they truly represented what he had earned.

Unknown to my wife and daughters, I slipped into an area of our basement and burned both of those awards, because I hadn't *really* earned them. I was afraid that the time might come when my own wife or children might one day discover them and think they were honorably won. Lest that happen, I destroyed the evidence, because they reminded me of an era when I went through the mechanics of gospel living—not real living, but only the motions. I let them put stars on my forehead and an award insignia on my lapel, but they were for complying with the mechanics, not for qualifying spiritually.

An Award Earned and Happiness

Contrast that experience, if you will, with another experience that same night. As I continued to clean out records and books, I stepped over to the closet where some materials were located, and, as I opened the closet, in the shadows I could see my old high school letterman sweater hanging there. I took it out and, because I suppose this is the human side of people, put it on. It was a bit snug here and there. (I didn't dare let my family see me in it for fear they wouldn't understand.)

I stood in front of the mirror. There in front was the big block *H* from Hollywood High, and it had some interesting insignia attached that signified that I was somebody—some white stripes on beautiful maroon background on the left sleeve. I stood there with real pride. I thought, "Isn't that great!" Do you know why? Because I had really earned my letter, and that letterman's sweater still has a significant place in my heart.

Let me tell you why. During the 1942 baseball season we had a real contest going in the Western Athletic Association. Hollywood High, my team, and Fairfax High, our arch rivals, were battling it out for the city championship. We came to the end of the season one game behind Fairfax. We had two games to go and, wouldn't you know, they both had to be played against Fairfax. I drew the starting assignment to pitch the second-to-the-last game. Well, I had the usual butterflies. You know how it is—I couldn't sleep; I couldn't think; I couldn't study; I couldn't do anything.

Coach Meb Schroeder Teaches Great Lesson

The day before the crucial game, Coach Meb Schroeder had us all assembled on the ball field. As we stood around the batting cage getting last-minute instructions and the old pep talk, we were reminded of the standards and the oaths we had taken as athletes earlier in the year. (Schroeder held a very tight rein and demanded high standards. We had each committed ourselves to no smoking, no drinking, and no staying out late at night. He was building character in boys, not just teams or statistics. We took that commitment, and each of us promised we would obey —and we knew the penalties if we disobeyed.)

As he made his way around the circle that day on the field, he happened to glance over to where Jimmy, our star second baseman, was standing. He was the Maury Wills of our team; he was the take-charge guy; he was the one who, when you had two men on base and only one out and things really were falling apart, could mold the team together.

The coach said, "Jimmy, is that a nicotine stain on your finger?"

Jimmy said, "Yes, sir."

He said, "Don't you know the rule?"

"Yes, sir."

He said, "Do you know the penalty?"

"Yes."

"You see the gym?"

"Yes, sir."

"Turn in your uniform right now. You are through!"

The team was stunned. I almost hollered, "Coach, wait until tomorrow! We've got a game to win, and we need Jimmy!" Isn't that the way we sometimes look at it? It doesn't matter what we are doing to people, but let's just win!

I have never seen a more dejected figure than Jimmy that day as he walked toward the gym. But Schroeder was the kind of coach who didn't let a boy flounder. He worked with him all the more, even though he had lost his privilege to be on the team.

The next day on the Fairfax diamond we went into the bottom half of the thirteenth inning before they squeezed across run number one, which was the deciding run that beat us. I bawled all night! That was a heartbreaker for any pitcher to lose.

Twenty years have come and gone, and what is interesting about life is that I don't remember who was on top of the standing those many years ago, who batted what, where, when, but I do remember a great coach who taught me to discipline myself.

Principles, Standards, and True Happiness

So as I occasionally look in the closet and see my letterman's sweater, I say, "Thank you, Meb Schroeder, for letting me know that the real important things in life are principles and standards—not records." This is what

I have found true happiness to be. It is great to win, but it's still greater to find the joy and peace and serenity that come in truly living standards and principles of the gospel. I think that is what the scriptures are all about, and when applied to the everyday things of life, true joy is experienced.

Happiness Is . . .

Happiness is knowing that if you will apply these things in all you do, blessings of heaven will come.

Happiness is being able to travel throughout the Church and to see people who have caught this vision.

Happiness is knowing that God really lives, that Jesus is the Christ, and that a prophet is on the earth today.

Happiness, to me, is knowing that these things are true.

CHAPTER 9

Have Ye Inquired of the Lord?

One day when I boarded a plane in Boston, I saw one of our returned missionaries on his way home from Europe. (You can always recognize returned missionaries —they have a certain something that identifies them.) When I made my way back to the part of the plane where he was seated, I noticed that the seat next to him was not yet occupied. So I asked if I could sit with him.

Not recognizing me and considering me to be a potential investigator, he said, "Please." And before the plane had taken off, he leaned over and said, "Sir, what do you know about the Mormons?"

I said, "I know a little bit."

"Would you like to know more?"

And I did, so I said, "Yes, I would."

He whipped out that flannelboard quicker than I have ever seen, and the next five hundred miles I got the first four discussions. He did such a fine job that I didn't have the heart to tell him who I was. But I want him to know wherever he is that I am grateful to be an associate. I'll always be grateful for good effective teachers.

Charles B. Stewart

One of the great teachers who walked into my life when I was a priest was Charles B. Stewart, the father of Ike Stewart, president of the Tabernacle Choir. I suppose Brother Stewart was in his late seventies when he was assigned by the bishop of the Hollywood Ward to be our adviser. And you know what a seventy-year-old man looks like to sixteen-year-olds. We thought Moses had returned, and we weren't about to give him much of a chance. We soon learned to love and respect him for his teaching ability. He loved us and we knew it.

A New Thought

I'll never forget the first morning we went to our priests class. Brother Stewart was standing at the door—not in the room—greeting his boys. He stopped us one by one as we made ready to enter, and when it came my turn, he said, "You're Paul Dunn, aren't you?"

"Yes, sir."

Then he told me a little bit about myself. "Now," he said, "we have a requirement in this class. You can't enter until you give me a new thought. Have you got one?"

I hadn't had a new thought in ten years, but he insisted, "We want a new thought."

When I couldn't give him one, he said, "All right, I'll teach you one. Now you repeat after me, 'Attention is the mother of memory.' "

I stumbled through it and said it back to him.

He said, "That's fine, young man. You may enter my class."

We had a fine class. I'll never forget how he used to seat us in a semicircle around his feet, and he would walk back and forth. When we would get out of order, he would come along the row and say, "Now, young men, we have invited the Lord to be with us today and He expects our attention. Remember, 'Attention is the mother of memory.'"

One day he came down the row and said, "You realize, young men, that you are the future leaders of the Church. Why, in this very circle," he continued, "there may be a future General Authority."

"Yeah, yeah! We know!" we used to say.

Well, the class period ended, and as we went out, he stopped me at the door and said, "You can't leave until you give me another new thought."

I still didn't have one, and so he taught me another. He said, "Remember, Paul, 'A strong man and a waterfall always channel their own path.' Now repeat it back to me."

And when I did, he said, "You may go."

The following week I came to class, and once more he said, "Do you have another new thought?"

"No, sir."

So he taught me another.

Example sheds a genial ray which men are apt to borrow,
So first improve yourself today and then your friends
tomorrow.

I had a little trouble giving that one back, but he helped me. Later as the class ended, and he said, "Have you got a new thought?"

"No, I haven't."

"I'll teach you another," he said.

There was a wise old owl that sat in an oak.
The longer he sat the less he spoke.
The less he spoke the more he heard.
Oh! Why can't we be like that wise old bird?

He called these sayings "gem thoughts," and told us

that the time would come in our lives when we would want
to draw upon these ideas to help us.

"Paul," he would say, " 'A good name is better than a
girdle of gold.' Remember that!"

Well, we finally graduated from his class after almost
two years of association, and I can testify to you of the
impact because his example still remains.

I was on the island of Okinawa in May 1945 when I
received a letter from Mrs. Stewart, and attached to the
letter was a little obituary column announcing the passing
of Charles B. Stewart, my adviser, friend, and teacher.
And honor to his name, in his concluding week of life he
had typed a fresh page of "gem thoughts" for one of his
priests who was fighting a great war far away. I still carry
that page with me. And so I admonish you to listen carefully to your leaders and teachers. Such is the impact of
great personalities.

Keep Learning

I know some of you get a little discouraged at times
when things aren't always going just the way they should
—pressures of the moment, great decisions to make, lots
of other complications—but listen while you can, because
I promise you the hour will come in your life when you
will draw upon great words as you make important decisions in your life.

I remember walking across the University of Southern California campus some years ago and entering a
building where I noticed a great thought engraved over
the door in cement. It said: "I am still learning," and it
was signed, "Michelangelo." That is a humbling thought
to me, and I take great comfort in it because it is a basic
part of the gospel program.

Aristotle said, "It is not the possessions but the desires of men that must be equalized, and this is impossible unless they have a sufficient education."

Robert Hutchins, another great mind of our era, made this statement: "True education is the improvement of men through helping them learn to think for themselves." A great teacher, a great mind, helps a student to get along without his teacher, not to become dependent upon him. I like that philosophy very much, and I encourage you to develop the habit of collecting good thoughts.

Here is what Abraham Lincoln said about learning: "Nothing is more terrible than ignorance in action."

Shakespeare put it another way: "'Tis the mind that makes the body rich."

Socrates said, "Let him that would move the world first move himself." I have discovered that we are our own stumbling blocks in life.

Mortimer Adler put it another way: "Man's greatness lies in this power of thought."

Wonderful as these thoughts are, they are not enough. Thoughts of good people help to motivate us, but it is the Lord we must consult for real answers.

"Have Ye Inquired of the Lord?"

There is an interesting statement in 1 Nephi 15:8, wherein the brothers of Nephi are contending with him as they frequently did. They had just experienced difficulty in interpreting their father's dream of the olive tree and the branches and were disturbed because they did not quite understand it. So they approach Nephi for an interpretation, and Nephi gives very excellent counsel. He says in one single line: "Have ye inquired of the Lord?"

A Personal Crisis

Could I make modern application of that, as we contemplate life, as we find ourselves in the midst of great struggles, as we experience life. Could I suggest: "Have ye inquired of the Lord?" Therein rests the total answer to all the problems that mankind faces. It is vital that we know our Heavenly Father and His real nature. Many are confused as to who and what He is.

Many of our friends in other faiths find somewhat of a personal crisis as they attempt to inquire of the Lord. God, for so many, is too distant or is not fully understood. Too often the omnipotence is stressed to such an extent that he becomes unreachable. This coupled with the teaching of the depravity of man, the sinner, the worthless being tends to stress the gap between God our Father and His offspring.

On the other hand through modern-day prophets and through our own experiences, we have found that God is literally our Heavenly Father. We are His offspring, the greatest accomplishment of His creation. He continually reveals Himself to us through the prophets in order that we might be like Him. We, being His children, are striving to be more like Him. The Latter-day Saints stress the closeness of God and man. It is because of this understanding that daily communication with the Lord plays such a vital role. It becomes easy then to follow the counsel of Nephi when he asks: "Have ye inquired of the Lord?" Therein rests the answer to all the problems that mankind faces.

Concept of an Eternal Father

There shouldn't be any question in this Church as to the true nature and concept of an Eternal Father. He is an Exalted Father in whose image we have been created. We are His children and He loves us.

There isn't a soul throughout the world about whom God does not care and care very much, and He hears and answers our prayers. That is my testimony to you. I know that God lives and that He can hear and answer prayers. I found that out on a beachhead some years ago when I followed the admonition of that great Book of Mormon leader Enos.

Learn to inquire of the Lord as Enos did.

Enos Inquires of the Lord

Enos went to hunt beasts one day. (I always like to think of him as a Nephite three-year letterman—a good athlete!) He tells us how the impressions his father made upon him sank deep into his heart and impressed his mind.

When he found himself alone, he knelt down to pray, and "all day long did he pray." Did you ever pray all day about a problem? Or are you just a fifteen-minute Latter-day Saint? Are you going to give the Lord just fifteen minutes to reveal His mind and will, or will you "pray all day and into the night," as did Enos if necessary. Do you want to know that much? Are you hungering and thirsting for answers sufficient to seek and knock so that you might find?

Then Enos records that the voice of the Lord came unto him saying that his sins had been forgiven and he would be blessed. Can you imagine the sweet peace that would come into your mind, hearing the voice of the Lord saying to you, "Paul (or James or Jean), thy sins are forgiven thee." Wouldn't that be a wonderful comfort?

A Missionary Inquires

There was an elder in the mission field who by all physical standards should not have gone on a mission. He was 80 percent deaf in one ear and 70 percent deaf in the other. He had a terrible speech impediment because he had never heard his own voice clearly. This elder was out playing touch football with the other missionaries of the district. A big 270-pound elder went up to block a pass, and this semi-deaf elder was underneath him. As the 270-pound elder came down, he crashed upon the other elder's head, causing instant total deafness.

His companion called me that night and said, "President Dunn, we have a problem. Elder _____ can't hear. He lost his hearing in a little accident today on the ball field."

So I suggested that they bring him to Cambridge, where we had excellent medical facilities and all the services of the Harvard Medical School. We put him in touch with two of the finest ear specialists, and after an extensive examination, the report came back, "He will not likely regain his hearing."

Then I brought the elder into my office to decide what was best to do for him. He could not hear me, and so we were writing notes to each other. As I was sharing with him some of my feelings, he wrote me a note that said, "You believe in God, don't you, President Dunn?"

And I wrote back, "Yes, Elder, you know I do."

Then he gave me in the next little note, almost verbatim, the counsel of Nephi, "Would you inquire of the Lord, because I came to serve a mission."

I wrote back, "Certainly."

So we knelt down together after I closed the door and locked it. I put my arm around his shoulder. He could only hear the prayer through the Spirit. I asked Heavenly Father to give me the strength and the courage and the know-how to touch the life of this young man.

I felt impressed during that prayer to give him a special blessing of health, and so we arose together. I seated him in a chair, placed my hands upon his head, and called upon Heavenly Father by the authority and power of the priesthood that I hold and in the name of our Savior, Jesus Christ.

I paused momentarily, and then as forcefully as I have ever felt an impulse from heaven, I promised him that he would hear again. Afterward we stood together and embraced each other with tears in our eyes.

Then he wrote back on a little note, "Send me back to my area. I'll be all right. The Lord has spoken to my soul."

I sent him back to New Hampshire. The next morning the telephone rang. "Hello, President Dunn. Just thought you'd like to know that I got my hearing back last night."

"Have ye inquired of the Lord?" Whatever your dilemma, I counsel you to take it to the Lord.

Effort Needed

I want to testify to you that God is real, that He hears us, that He is concerned about our welfare. But we have come to mortality to learn, to develop, to find, to seek, and sometimes it is pretty hard, but it is the only way we grow. Nothing worthwhile has ever come without effort, and I believe the Lord, knowing that, tries to keep the formula before us in order that we might seek, knock, and find.

I give you my witness that the Lord will answer if we will inquire.

CHAPTER 10

The "Ships" of Life

Some years ago I had the opportunity to serve as president of the New England Mission. New England is very special, inasmuch as it's the birthplace of our country and the birthplace of many of the great early leaders of this Church. Some forty-plus early contributors to the faith found their homes in New England. Three that are very prominent, of course, are the Prophet Joseph Smith, Brigham Young, and Oliver Cowdery. I was honored to be the caretaker—spiritually speaking—for a while of that great area.

Occasionally even mission presidents need motivation, and in New England I used to go up to the birthplace of the Prophet on occasion to renew spiritual feelings and commitments. I used to get a lift historically as well. Occasionally I'd drive eleven miles from the mission headquarters out to old Concord, where the North Bridge is located. This was the location of the Revolutionary War. As I would walk up and down the banks of the Concord River reminiscing about our early heritage, I would gain great strength.

Eleven miles in the other direction is Boston Harbor. Anchored to the moorings there is *Old Ironsides,* one of the great vessels of all time. This magnificent old ship, commonly known as the *USS Constitution,* did more, I suppose, than any other single vessel in preserving the freedom of this country during the War of 1812. Over seventy times it went to sea with our enemies and won every battle. It's still commissioned as one of the great ships of the United States Navy.

Old Ironsides was prepared all the time so that it could meet the challenging enemy. Our lives can be somewhat parallel with this great ship.

Workmanship

I'd like to stress the importance of anchoring what Adam S. Bennion called the five ships of life next to *Old Ironsides.* I would hope in your harbor that you would put next to the *USS Constitution* that first vessel *Workmanship.*

If I have one concern as I travel the United States and the world, it is in seeing sloppy workmen. I've just completed building a new home in Salt Lake City, and it's been quite revealing. One of the things that I noted is that there are very few workers today who take pride in their work. I was appalled at how many workers really didn't care about the quality of their work. They were in it for the dollar or "how quick I can get out of here today," and service seemed to be a forgotten product. I would hope and pray that we would learn to take pride in our work. The prefabricated home today is an outgrowth of poorly trained workmen. Craftsmen are becoming fewer!

I would hope that our years of life would be spent in preparing and learning to be great workmen, true craftsmen. The world needs quality in service and performance, for it seems to be a lost art. I wish that each person in this world would learn to do his job well by learning the tools of his trade.

It was James Truslow Adams who said, "There are

obviously two kinds of education: one teaches you how to make a living [that's the academic side to a great extent], the other how to live [the gospel]." Let's take pride in our work and not worry about a clock. Go the extra mile to get a task done the very best way you know how. The world needs your faith and many talents individually and collectively. Develop workmanship!

Friendship

Second in your fleet, I hope you would include that vessel *Friendship*. I notice as I travel the world that there are a lot of lonely people. I think we have enough scriptures in our standard works that indicate we ought to be concerned about our fellowmen.

The Savior put it very well when He said, "Lose yourself in the service of others." We have a tendency, because of our own insecurities, to become turned in, selfish, self-oriented. We're here on earth, in part, to learn how to turn ourselves out, to lose ourselves and help someone else, to relieve the frustrations of others. I would like to challenge all men and women in and out of this Church to befriend those who need a friend.

When my wife and I went back to Boston, we took with us our daughter Kellie. Our other two were attending the university, and so we went from a family of five to a family of three in one evening. Kellie became an only child overnight—quite a frustration and a challenge. Then, to top it off, we moved to a new area, and she was lonesome for her friends and her acquaintances at school.

We signed her up in a school in Cambridge that was built in 1888. The school had lots of weeds in the yard, and a terrible musty smell greeted one as he entered the building. Even the floorboards buckled, and you got an eerie feeling as you walked the halls.

We tried to prepare Kellie for her first day at school

just as soon as we arrived. Because the beginning of the fall term was yet in the future, she didn't panic, but as the day drew closer, her concern increased. We took her shopping for new school clothes and had a family evening organized around how to adjust and what to do and how to turn yourself out to adjust to the new environment. She could handle that all right because it was still theory. Then the night before we planned a special program around helping her for the special day.

She retired to her bed but seemed quite restless. The next few hours passed, and she suddenly appeared at the door where I was studying. She was rubbing her stomach and said, "Dad, I'm sick." I knew what kind of sickness she had—not physical, not mental, but emotional.

So I invited her over, put her on my lap, and we chatted for a moment. Then I put on some music that we liked to listen to together and rubbed her tummy. She finally drifted into Never-Never Land and seemed pretty well under control. I took her sleepy body, with its dangling legs, upstairs and put her back in bed.

I turned to go out, got as far as the door, and she said, "I'm still awake." I went back and lay down on the bed and stroked her head for a few moments until she finally went to sleep.

The next morning while I was at breakfast, she came down dressed only in her slip. She said, "Dad, I just thought you ought to know that I don't think I'll go to school today."

I said, "Why not?"

She said, "I think I'm going to throw up."

I knew what she was trying to tell me. "I'm nervous. Will my teachers like me? Will I be accepted?" Oh, she was not capable of asking those kinds of questions, but those were the concerns of her heart. She was lonely, and she didn't know how to fit in. She was concerned about making new friends.

I said, "Well, you know the answer to that, don't you?"

"Yes, sir, I guess we're going." We went.

I said, "How would you like your mother and me to drive you over?" She liked that, and so we did.

We got in front of the school, and the tears started to well up. The warning bell sounded, and I tried to get her out of the car. She grabbed hold of my leg like a tackle would, and I had to literally drag her to the door. I opened the door, and then she clung to both legs.

I'll never forget the expression on the face of that eight-year-old when she looked at me and said, "Dad, if you really love me, if you really do, you won't send me in there."

I said, "Honey, this may sound like a strange philosophy, but it's because I do love you that I am sending you in there."

We went in. The tears really came without shame. Then a little miracle happened. Around the corner came the only other Latter-day Saint in the whole student body. She had seen Kellie a couple of times at some stake functions, and this little girl was an extrovert's extrovert. Even though only eight, she had learned to lose herself in the interest of others.

She came around the corner and said, "Oh, Kellie! How are you? Gosh, it's good to see you! What's your home room number?" And Kellie told her.

"Great!" she said. "That's mine too. Come on, I'll show you where."

Before Kellie knew it, she had let go and walked about ten paces out in front of me. Then she turned and said, "Oh, Dad, you can go now. I don't need you anymore."

We need friends, and the Latter-day Saint people with

their philosophy ought to be the friendliest in the world. I'd like to challenge everyone to extend this tremendous influence to the rest of the world. Learn to develop friendship.

Courtship

Hopefully, next to friendship you'll anchor the vessel *Courtship*. This is a great ship. But if I have one concern as your friend, it is that sometimes we think that just one Church member's marrying another member guarantees eternal happiness and solves all problems. You don't have to look very far in our society to see that there is more to mate selection than just membership in the Church. I hope you are considering the intellectual, the spiritual, and the emotional as well as the physical. I wouldn't want to minimize the physical—it's important to look right, to project yourself well—but those aren't the only things that build eternal joy and happiness.

I hope that women will go all the way with their education. Sometimes there's a challenge in becoming just a housewife. Women need a spiritual and intellectual capability that will lift their husbands and complement them in terms of what the gospel teaches.

I appreciate that all education doesn't have to be formal. The Prophet Joseph Smith and many others are excellent examples of self-educated persons. But the glory of God is intelligence, and intelligence He expects us to use in mate selection. As the years progress, you will learn that spirituality plays a much greater role in family togetherness and solidarity than you now realize. It's the spirit that gives depth and dimension. I challenge you to create a never-ending courtship.

Hardship

I hope next to that ship *Courtship* you have anchored

the vessel *Hardship.* Now you wouldn't be worth much in this world if you didn't have a hardship or two. Sometimes young people would like to go through life without a challenge. They think it seems easier, but it isn't! The purpose of mortality is to learn to be like our Heavenly Father, and hardship is the refining tool that prepares us for that great and glorious day. We all have barriers, obstacles. I think the purpose of life is to see how we handle them, rather than whether or not we have them.

I had 467 full-time missionaries given to me over a period of three years. What a glorious experience! I remember I hadn't been in New England more than an hour when the telephone rang. On the line was an elder whom I hadn't yet met—an elder who had been in the mission field just one week. He had some concerns, as sometimes missionaries do, and wanted to go home.

He didn't just say, "I want to go home." He announced that he was going. He was a small man in stature, quite good-looking, and a good athlete. But he was born with a handicap, which was one of his barriers—he had a problem with his larynx. When he spoke, he spoke with a harsh voice, and people often made fun of him.

He announced on the phone, "President Dunn, I just called to tell you I'm going home tonight, so don't try to stop me."

I said, "Well, at least pay me the courtesy of coming over and getting acquainted and saying goodbye."

"All right," he said, "I'll come by on my way to the airport."

He came over. In the meantime I checked his file and found, among other things, one thing in my favor—he wanted to be an athlete. He was a good one too, and he wanted to make a career out of sports.

When he came, he said, "Now, President, you're not going to talk me into staying."

I said, "I don't intend to. Tell me your problem."

He said, "It's very simple. I don't have a testimony. I don't believe in the Lord. Furthermore, my home life hasn't been what it ought to be. I don't like my dad! I don't like my mother! I don't like this Church! I don't like this mission! And I already dislike you!"

"Thank you for your frankness," I said, "but let me tell you something. I don't know what all the circumstances are," I said, "but let me tell you something. The Lord lives, and He loves you. Your parents, for reasons you can't fully comprehend, love you. This Church loves you. This mission loves you. And I like you a little bit.

"Now," I said, "you can walk out of this mission anytime you want, but I don't think you're a quitter. You may have a lot of hang-ups and problems, but you're not a quitter. I noticed from your record that you don't quit.

"Let me tell you something you may not know. I played professional baseball for a number of years and found myself behind in early and middle innings of many a ball game. If you were my coach when we were behind five to two in the seventh inning and I came to you and said, 'Coach, let's get out of here while we can and save face,' what would you say?"

He said, "We've got two more innings to catch up and win."

I said, "Exactly, and a mission is no different!"

"Well," he said, "that's baseball."

I said, "Yes, and the game of life is played by the same rules and principles. I don't think you're going to quit, because you're just not that kind of player. There's the door. You can go if you must, but I don't think you will."

"Well," he said, "I'll try it one more week."

"Fine. One more week. You call me next week, and we'll talk about it."

He called me the next week, and he gave me the same dialogue. He didn't even miss a line. We had it out again, and would you believe for the next 103 weeks. Every week, through the mail, in person, or on the phone—"I'm going, President!"

"Thanks Elder, but I don't think you will."

Then the 104th week it happened. Another phone call came, and he said, "I've got to tell you. It happened! I got the Spirit!" And he told me of some very special experiences he had had that week—how the Lord had answered his prayers and how he received a testimony. Through real hardship and prayer, he received an answer.

The following Sunday he came into the mission home for his last evening prior to his departure home. We used to have a simple ceremony when a group departed, and when it came time for him to speak, he said, "Can I be frank, President?"

I said, "You haven't hesitated up to now. What do you want to tell us?"

He said, "You know what I found out this week? I found what a testimony is. I believe in the Lord. He lives and I love Him. I love my mom and dad. I love this Church. I love this mission. And I kind of like you."

So don't apologize for hardship. Hit it head on. Just remember—it was Bob Newhart who said, "Crises plus time equal humor." The greatest crises you face right now or will ever face, given a little time, will seem humorous under other circumstances. Keep a sense of humor in your life. Be balanced, and meet hardship with a "come on" attitude.

Worship

Anchor next to the other great vessels *Worship*. This is perhaps the greatest ship of all. The Lord tells us why worship is important:

And worship him that made heaven, and earth, and the sea, and the fountains of waters—

Calling upon the name of the Lord day and night, saying: O that thou wouldst rend the heavens, that thou wouldst come down, that the mountains might flow down at thy presence.

And it shall be answered upon their heads; for the presence of the Lord shall be as the melting fire that burneth, and as the fire which causeth the waters to boil.

O Lord, thou shalt come down to make thy name known. . . . (D. & C. 133:39-42.)

With these great ships of life, may you sail life's stormy seas in peace and happiness.

Index for Discovering the Quality of Success